Copyright © M Publishing 2014

All rights reserved

No part of this publication may be reproduced, stored in or introduced into a retrieval system, or transmitted, in any form, or by any means (electronic, mechanical, photocopying, recording, or otherwise) without the prior written permission of the copyright owner.

Proof-reading
Steve Allen
Uros Ivovic

Artwork
Milena
Filip Ivovic (pages 12-13; 56-57; 120-121)

Published by
M PUBLISHING

Printed by
Lightning Source, UK

A catalogue record for this book is available from the British Library

ISBN 978-1-909323-09-4

WORDS OF SILENCE

milena

M PUBLISHING

NOBODY'S NEVER

Must I know 8
Pondering 9
Stepping 10
Illusion 11
Maturing 12
Colours of night 13
Distance 14
Accept it 16
Confession 17
Round silence 18
Something is happening .. 20
Outside the window 21
Temptations 21

Discovery 23
Flow 24
Infinity 26
A riddle 28
Aching curiosity 29
A divine calling 30
To unknown me 33
I confess 34
Bubbles of silence 36
Dilemma 39
Destiny 40
Confession 42

SILENCE IS DIVINE

A circle 46
As sounds grow 47
Wind 48
Yellow silence 49
Integration 50
The house of secrets 51

Getting closer 53
Synthesis 53
Matured 54
Supper 54
I recognise 56
My silence 57

WAKE UP !

Be! 60
This moment 60
Real destination 62
Here and now 63
Questioned 64
Reliable companion 64

Choiceless 66
Encouragement 66
There is a sea 67
O, Endlessness! 68
Prayer 75

RUSSIAN CHIMES

Present and absent 80
Call 81
On the boat 82
Russian chimes 83
Ukraine 84

Inevitability 85
Russia 86
A posteriori 86
Replica 87

CONTENTS

I AM DISAPPEARING
KNOWING NOT WHERE YOU ARE

The end of summer 90
I shall tell you 91
Comes your non-coming .. 92
Pain 95
Longing 96
Come 97
Inner fire 97
Sparkles 99
Whirlpool 99
Being 100
You 102
Helpless 104

A wish 106
Dawn 109
Phoenix 111
The real 111
Song of dead birds 112
Dead game 112
Best view 115
Realisation 115
Eventually 117
Night visit 118
You are me 120

DEAR LORD ...

What else can I do 124
Your presence 124
Touch 127
Waking up 127
Essence knowing 128
Getting closer 128
Sacred place 131
Cosmic homeland 132
Programme 132
Tears 135
Direct experience 137
Inspirator 138
All of all 138
Remind me 140
Inner smile 140
Magician 142
Common name 142

Approaching 145
Lessons 145
Uniqueness 146
Life-giver 146
What and where 149
Sovereign 150
Omnipresent 153
Reflection 154
Single relationship 156
Oneness 159
You are the essence 160
Supreme mastery 162
I see you invisible 165
Diving into this moment 167
Somebody 168
Devoted to you 170
The last question 173

NOBODY'S NEVER

MUST I KNOW

Something organic is happening to me,
with years' strong drive
and conviction.

Where is this flow heading to?
I am all ears!

The night, deep and calm.

I feel the Universe whispering in my cells,
overwhelming me entirely
by its inconceivability.

It searches for me
and has me perpetually,
whilst I remain silent on its behalf.

Myself – a toy or a god?

PONDERING

Sunk in silence
I penetrate
the sticky landscapes
of thoughts unuttered.

I listen,
I observe.

From within nothingness,
I sense allness.

I seek and move
towards my completed self –
the one beyond time
the one beyond non-existence.

In a glass of water
– soundlessness.

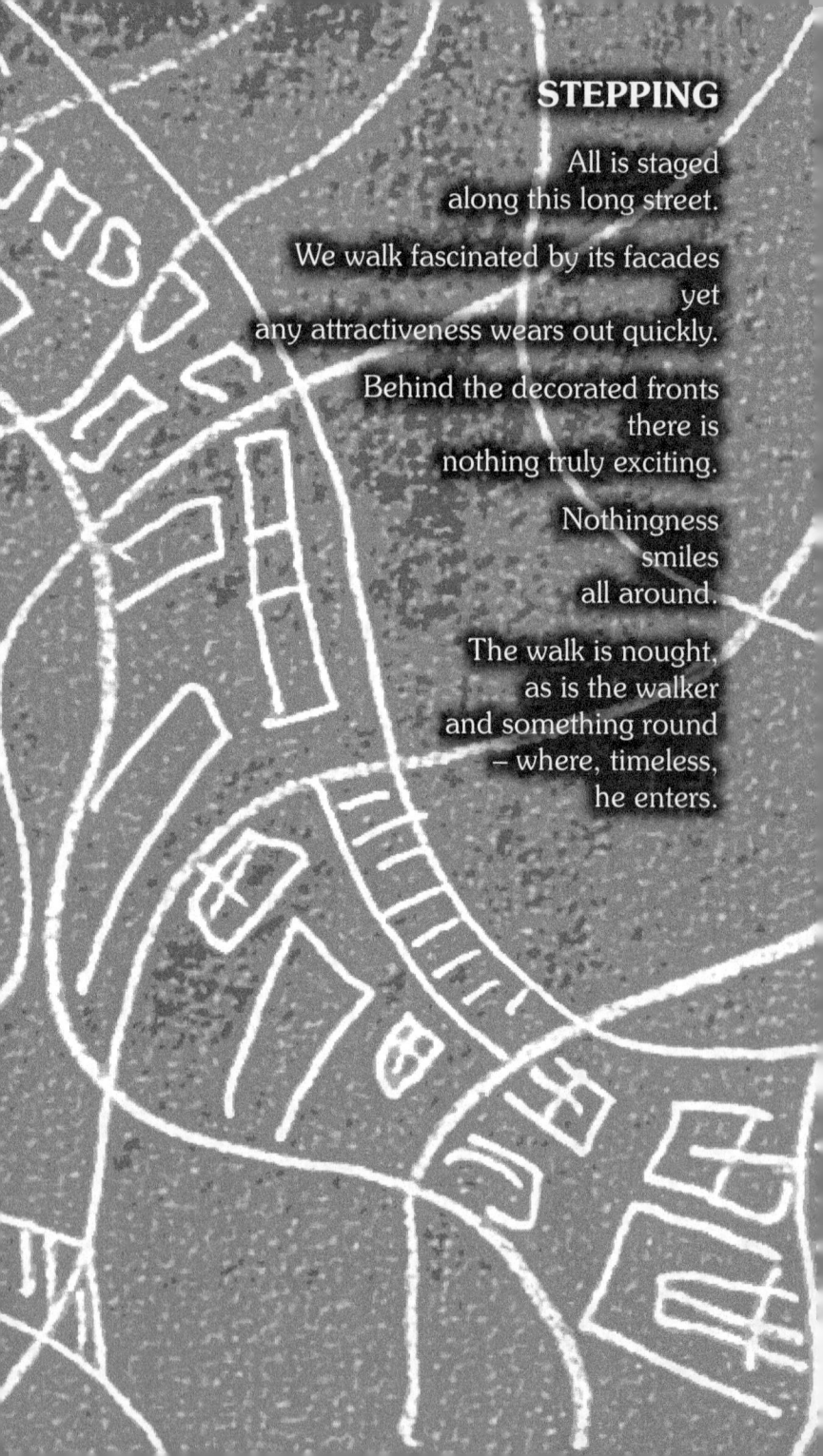

STEPPING

All is staged
along this long street.

We walk fascinated by its facades
yet
any attractiveness wears out quickly.

Behind the decorated fronts
there is
nothing truly exciting.

Nothingness
smiles
all around.

The walk is nought,
as is the walker
and something round
– where, timeless,
he enters.

ILLUSION

My arm,
elongated from a blue sleeve,
and my pen and my hair –
all are a mantle of an invisible energy,
a 3-dimensional performance
played out
by what is hidden behind.

There is no arm,
no sleeve, no hair.

There is no room,
table or pen.
Only certain vibrations cross
at the coordinates of solid matter
and a convincing illusion of the REAL
weaves its net.

Tonight,
I salute all the spirits
that are helping me.

MATURING

I am not asleep.

Silent,
I listen to a story in my bones:
am I accepting its meanings
or running away from them –
where to and for how long more?

It hurts.

The room is cold.
I feel emptiness,
and that rambling is harsh.

Where do the father
and the mother
fit in this all?

My mother!
Her child has grown up.

COLOURS OF NIGHT

When the darkness of night
swallows each being
spreading around
its cosmic magnitude –
I feel helpless.

It is a setting that captures me
without my consent.
I remain naked before myself,
losing even those comforting,
rose-tinted, lenses.

If I try to run away,
I will be mistaken.

The path of expectations
eventually curves back –
running away is completed by returning.

Hence, I cannot escape from my essence –
from the scales of its colours
that wait to be activated –
like musical notes longing to be played.

I cannot stop colours
within the darkness of night
from communicating with my essence.

DISTANCE

So many days
from human to human –
but only one glance!

ACCEPT IT

We – divided into days and given away,
with no power to fully explain meanings!
We – confused by many possible directions!

Is matter wastefully combined
into the formula of my genes,
tested and supervised over countless times?

Quiet, I live this answer
that is winded up
into a skein of time.

CONFESSION

Tonight,
a resignation
and acceptance of everything
dwells in my eyes,
and certain infinity
is soundlessly dragging me away
to itself.

ROUND SILENCE

The deep night silence,
before the first birdsongs,
reigns over the space.

One with this tranquillity,
I need no sound nor colour.

I am closing the circle.

It is the ultimate target of everything –
contentment of a circle!

19

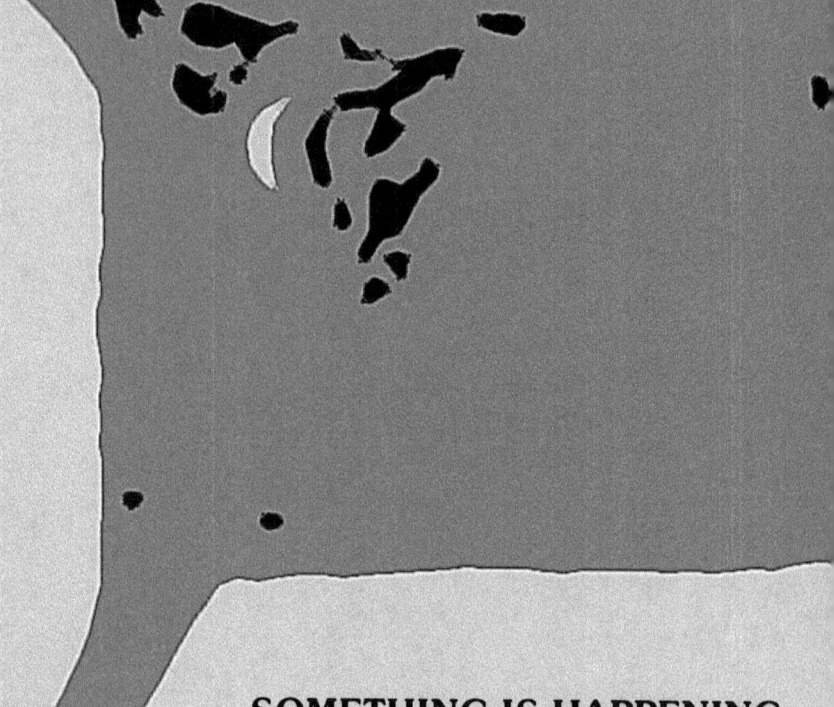

SOMETHING IS HAPPENING

It is cold and dark behind the window.
I sit for hours on end without moving
and get distorted by a rush of old thoughts.

The skipped trivialities attack me a hundred-fold
Only my eyes are open but there are no words.

I become all and I lose myself.

We are neither lungs nor footsteps.

We are something rolling
yet never launched on.

OUTSIDE THE WINDOW

The night is calm, clear, pierced by the silver moonlight.
Absorbing its breath, I grow many concerns;
uneasiness enters my heart.

The path to myself is strenuous.
I do not ask trees to walk
since it will not help.

I used to be afraid of fear but not anymore.
It recoiled under the twinkle of the faraway stars.

How much pettiness in everyday reality!
How much light in a day
yet – daylight does not reveal all!

Thoughts
through the window,
always!

TEMPTATIONS

This night and I
are silent together.

Each of my thoughts
stops at the edge of fears.

I need strength,
a lot of it.

Whom shall I ask, and what shall I ask?

PERDURABO !

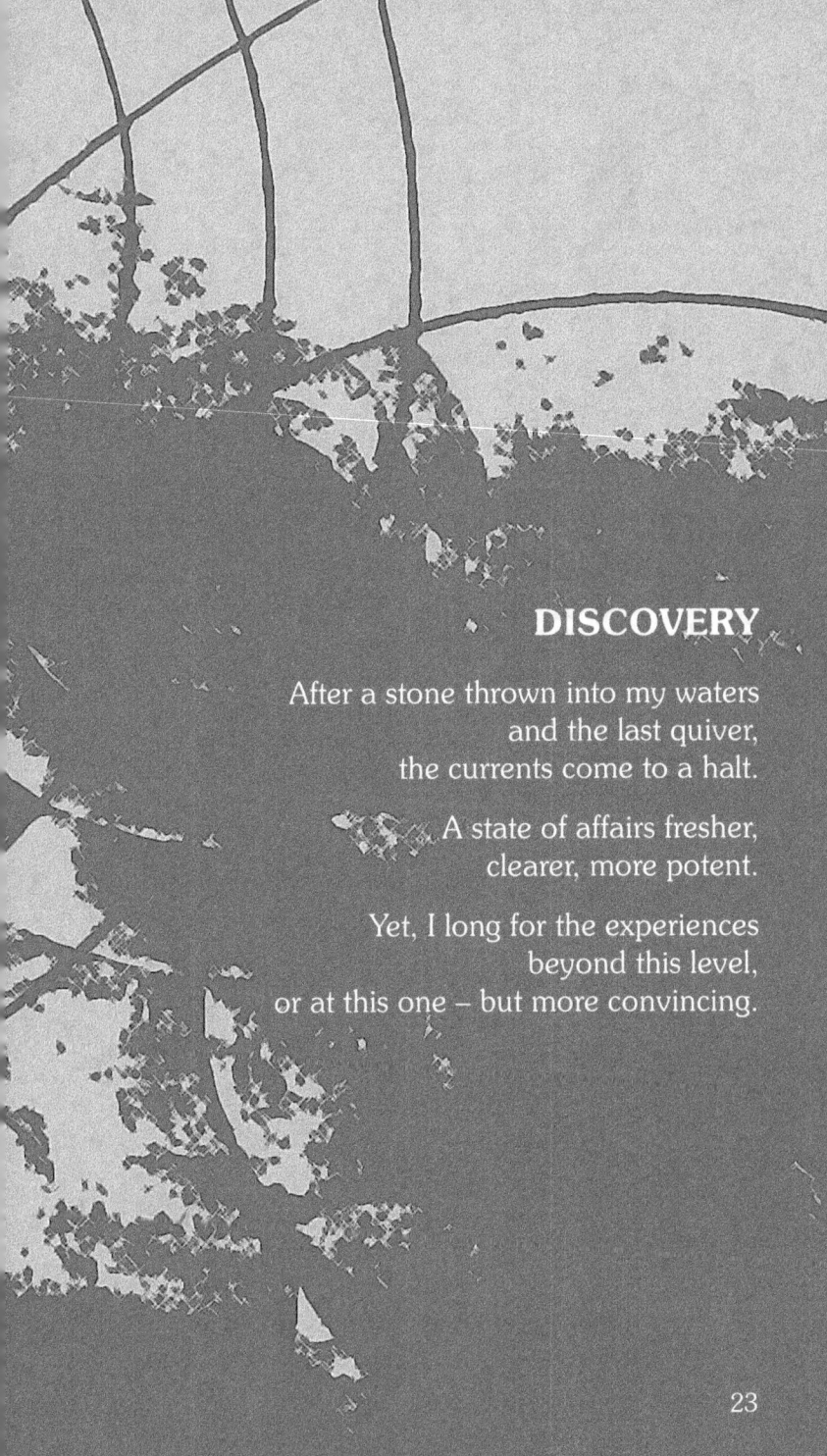

DISCOVERY

After a stone thrown into my waters
and the last quiver,
the currents come to a halt.

A state of affairs fresher,
clearer, more potent.

Yet, I long for the experiences
beyond this level,
or at this one – but more convincing.

FLOW

A bulk is sliding down.
Silently thawing, it converts into events.

Processes warn, the movement is dual,
multiplies breathing.
Need I say I am not afraid?

Soon I am beautifully my own.
A little, always a little towards something!

That tomorrow, which inspires this hour:
to know the words brother, mother, father, friend,...
to live for all things and enlarge the joy!

Flows the river,
awaited by a great calm sea.

INFINITY

Coming from this night's calm,
its depth and call,
thoughts on infinity
are dragging me.

Is there an end?
– Yes, as a temporary state
in the development of a thing!
– Yes, as a change
in the quality of its existence,
and the commencing of a new cycle!

Our life is a walk
towards an apparent end –
a game of hide-and-seek from it,
while advancing
from primeval shapes.

For the beginning to happen,
something has to be completed first.

Such thresholds are points
of physical and mental space,
where infinities open
towards endless directions
and get fertilised
by our choices.

Tonight,
I breathe at one of those points,
excited by the freedom
and creativity
divinely bestowed on me.

A RIDDLE

Little will change.
We shall go restless,
exalted,
everybody's
but never to arrive.

Owing ourselves?
To whom?
To this time,
or to an eternal tranquillity?

Which of our shapes
do we flow to?

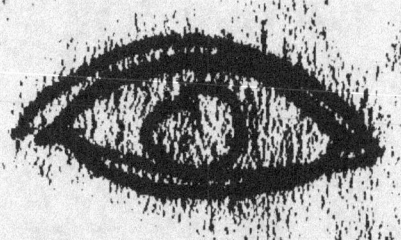

ACHING CURIOSITY

There is somebody
present in this body,
– a being dwelling.

This I is at pains,
in search of itself.

Will it forever remain an effort,
intense and uncertain?

Shall this I
expect itself from others
or
a pleasant echo from them
is enough?

A DIVINE CALLING

My dear divine potential,
I can feel you
calling me
from beyond,
waking me up
for new infinities!

I admire your faith
in this terrestrial me,
your intent to UNITE
and grow together –
while events go through us,
days hurry up,
time vanishes,
and we continue walking.

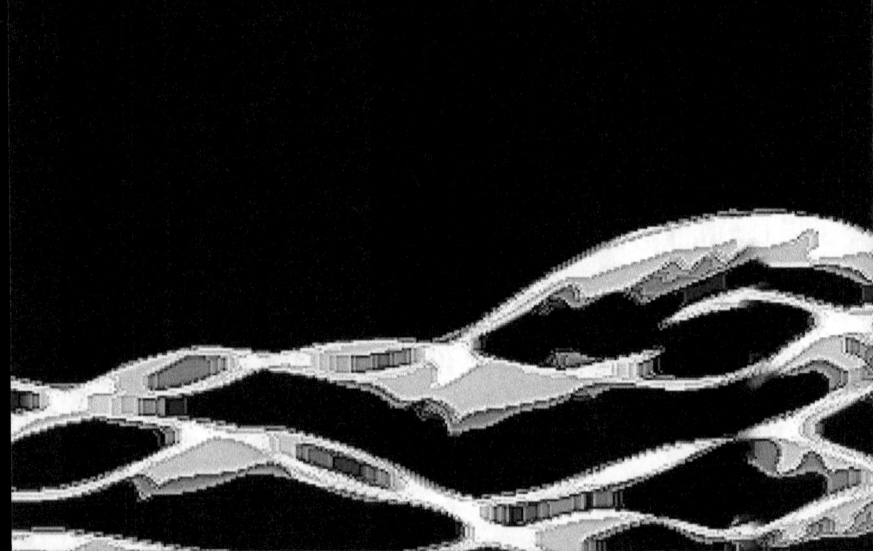

TO UNKNOWN ME

Do love me, my unknown part of me,
because without your love
fields are not that green.

Do love me, you, unknown part of me,
invisible scene of my visible being
where waves of my passion move
forced by the vigour of your invisibility.

Be loyal to me, my unknown part of me,
because without you
even this visible me
will lose its meaning.

I CONFESS

I would like to be
calmly calmed,
with no wish,
with no glance,
with intentions nonexistent,
with a formless form,
without echo,
invisible,
immaterial…
not even my own.

Nobody's, never
but an intention
within the Lord's Mind!

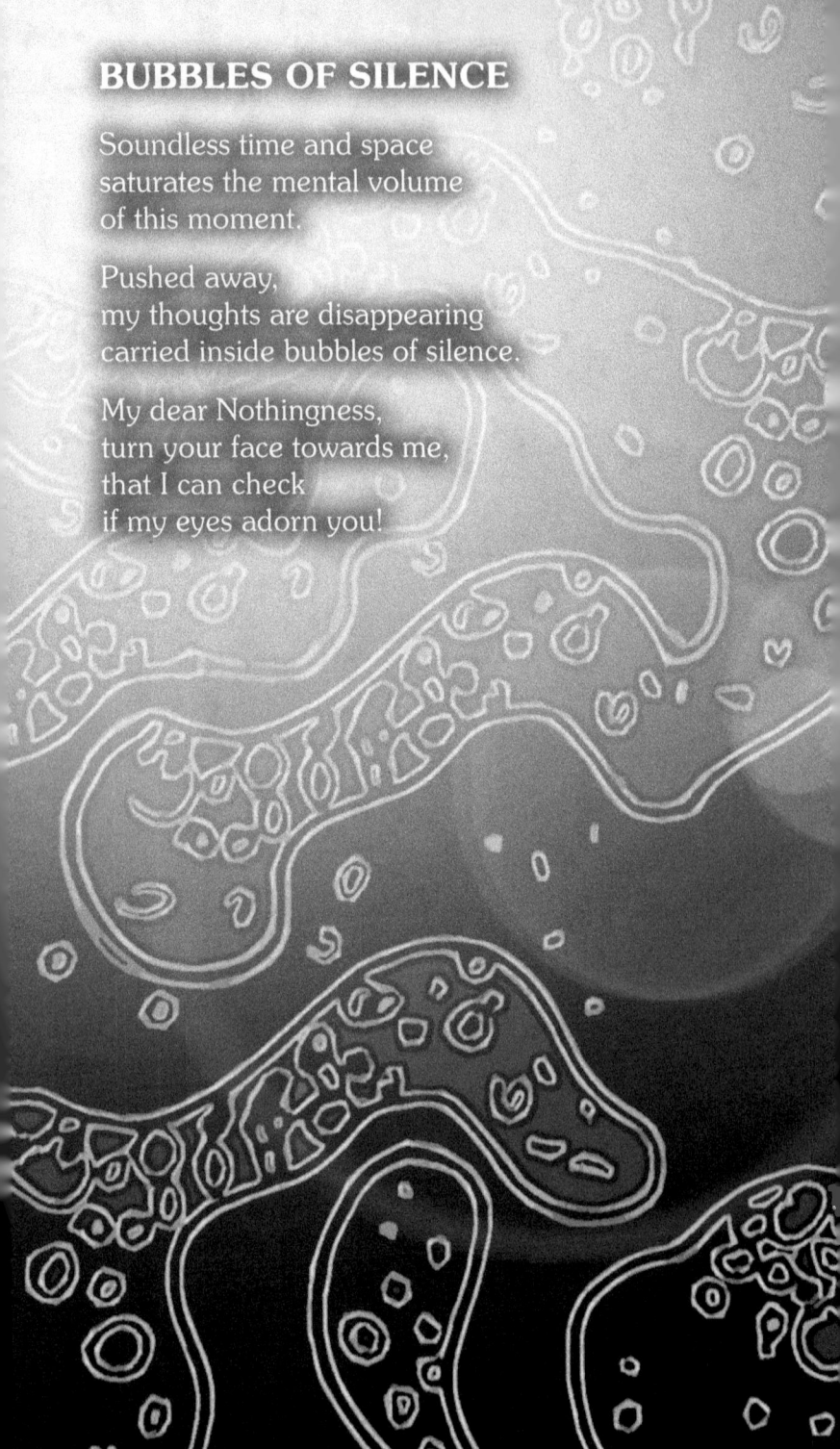

BUBBLES OF SILENCE

Soundless time and space
saturates the mental volume
of this moment.

Pushed away,
my thoughts are disappearing
carried inside bubbles of silence.

My dear Nothingness,
turn your face towards me,
that I can check
if my eyes adorn you!

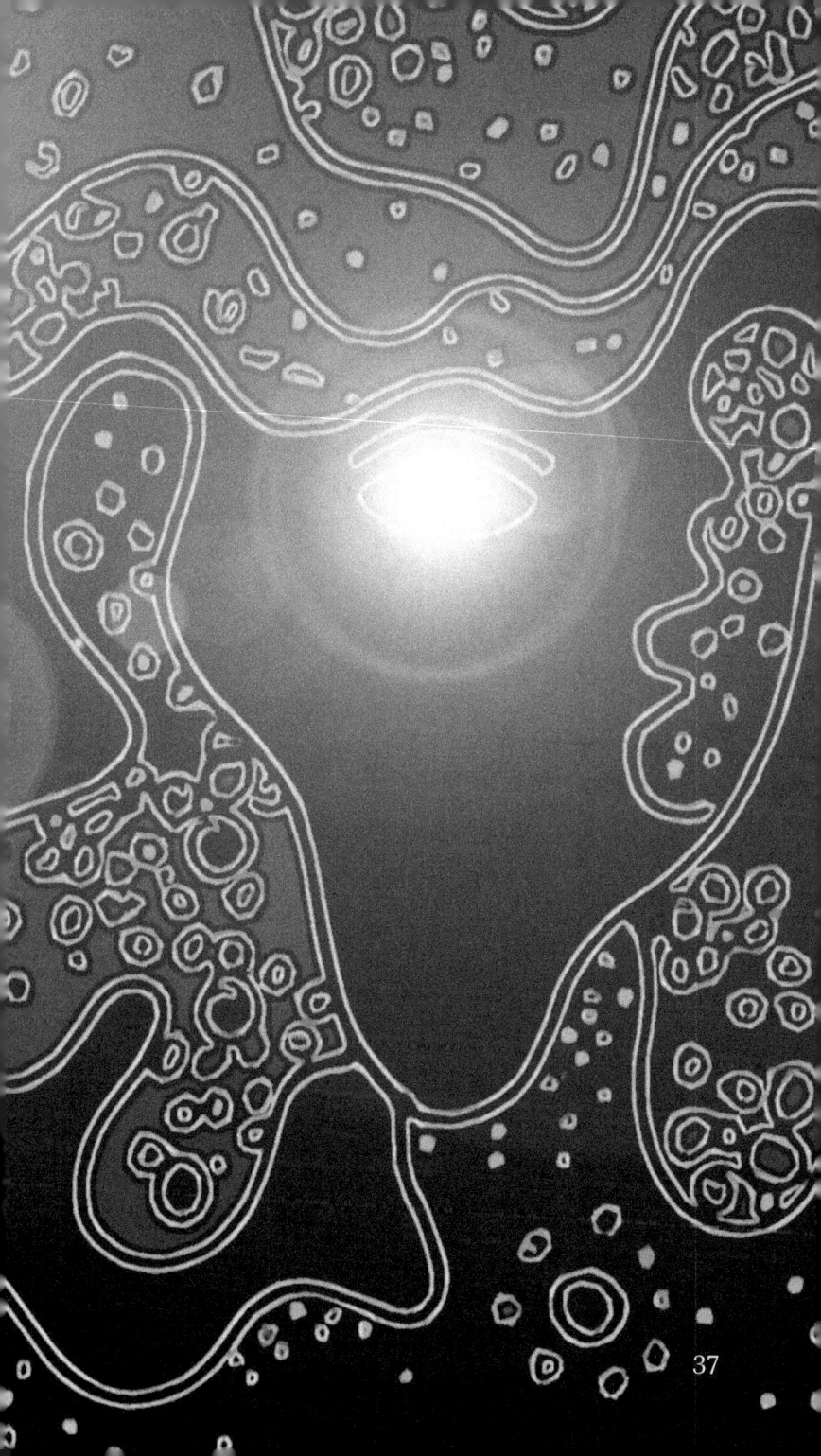

37

DILEMMA

Touched by sound, I opened
and on its waves started to flow.

And here is no me,
inside me, any more.

Wandered off,
am I looking for myself
or am I already that
what I try to find and be:
a glowing composite of energy,
which continuously ascends
its own awareness.

DESTINY

Today I breathe with ease,
conciliatorily clear,
uncompromisingly calm
and mine to the bone.

There is nobody there,
nobody to think of me
and nobody
to get in touch with me.

I shall grow and mature
to release my essence,
and let it serve
the Divine Orders on this planet.

CONFESSION

I AM
an immense desire
for beauty
and perfection;
a resolute belief
in them.

SILENCE IS DIVINE

A CIRCLE

Silently walking,
I skip a cloud full of rain,
a slight hesitation, a pain…

And I see, further still,
yet clearer!
A field of dandelions, a cricket –
we shall run together,
all the way to the white lilacs
in the streets of my childhood,
to the wet sand cookies on the riverbank.

Woods, songs, people!
I hurry back to myself.

AS SOUNDS GROW

I have a feeling:
I am going to fly!
Not even Earth
shall have me

I swear on my vision
that I shall be –
be through the now
and through that
which I shall bring.

I swear by my rapture
that I shall not let it down.

(You, the being inside me,
do you love yourself enough?
We are to survive!)

I need to keep my focus,
longer and stronger,
calm and committed –
to hear and continue the sounds
which are nearing.

Listen, sing along, and follow me!

WIND

Some days I shall catch the wind –
maybe at a summer's noon
full of colours.

Wind, your changes do not bother me!
The only transmutation that pains
is mine.

YELLOW SILENCE

Autumn is coming.

I feel comfortable at the thought
of fresh yellow mornings
and the wind swollen with stolen leaves.

The season of cold,
of search for a shelter within myself,
of intent tied up to my breathing.

Rain on the window
and fog in the hand.

We are the same quietness
that endures over time.

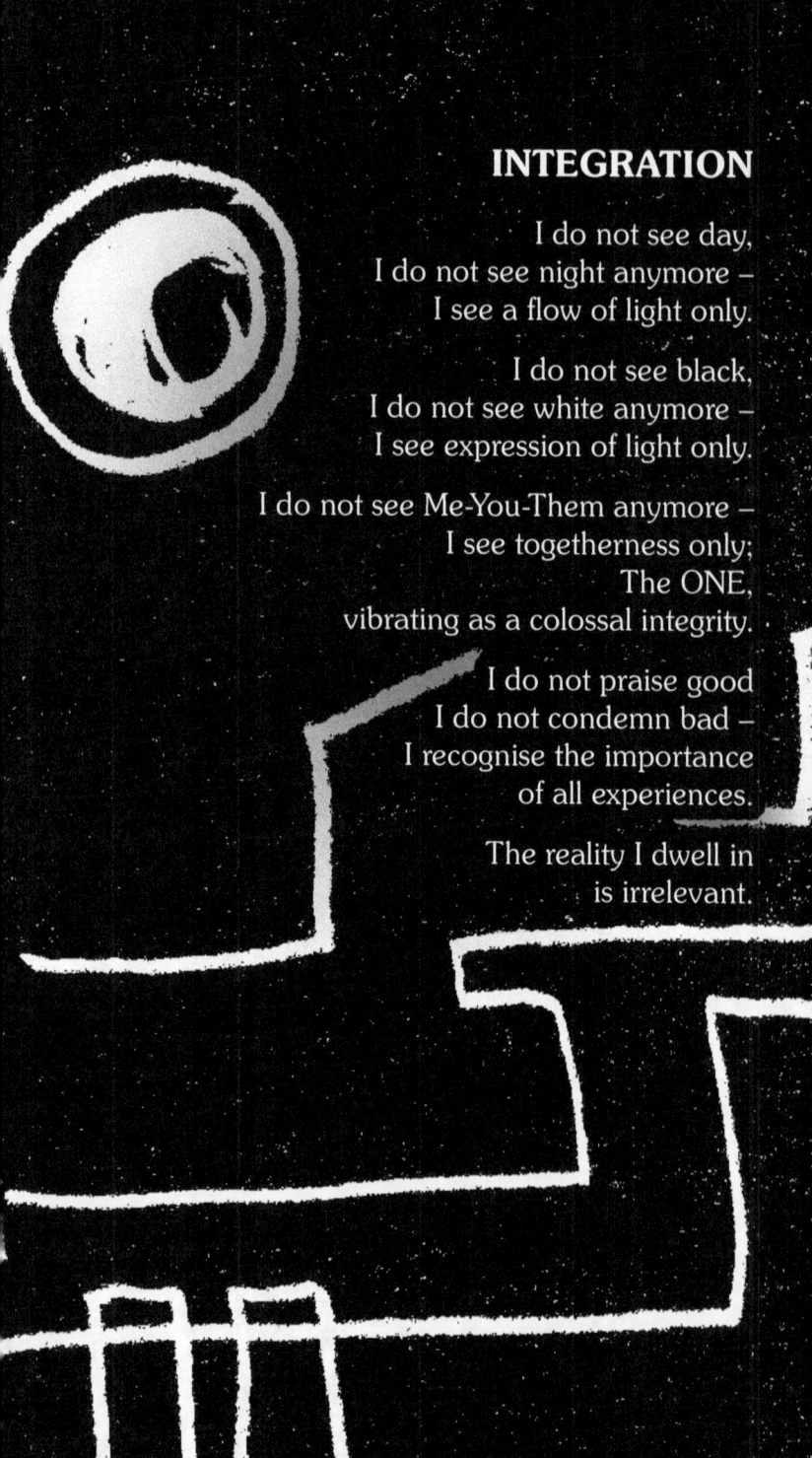

INTEGRATION

I do not see day,
I do not see night anymore –
I see a flow of light only.

I do not see black,
I do not see white anymore –
I see expression of light only.

I do not see Me-You-Them anymore –
I see togetherness only;
The ONE,
vibrating as a colossal integrity.

I do not praise good
I do not condemn bad –
I recognise the importance
of all experiences.

The reality I dwell in
is irrelevant.

THE HOUSE OF SECRETS

Autumn is grabbing my sleeve,
and waking me up
with the splendour
of its yellowness,
sharp freshness of sky
and clear, far away stars.

I transmute yellow into thought
and shift mental boundaries.
Soundless fog is no obstacle.

Day by day,
people are a new form of life,
of human, to me –
closer yet less comprehensible.

I feel my going into a house,
one time only, alone –
the house
the children do not know about.
One leaves it without this body.

I love nobody
but all are dear to me.
I feel good
but that doesn't please me.

I want something else!

I love leaves on the street,
hands in warm pockets,
distant lights...

All will come,
though, not sooner.

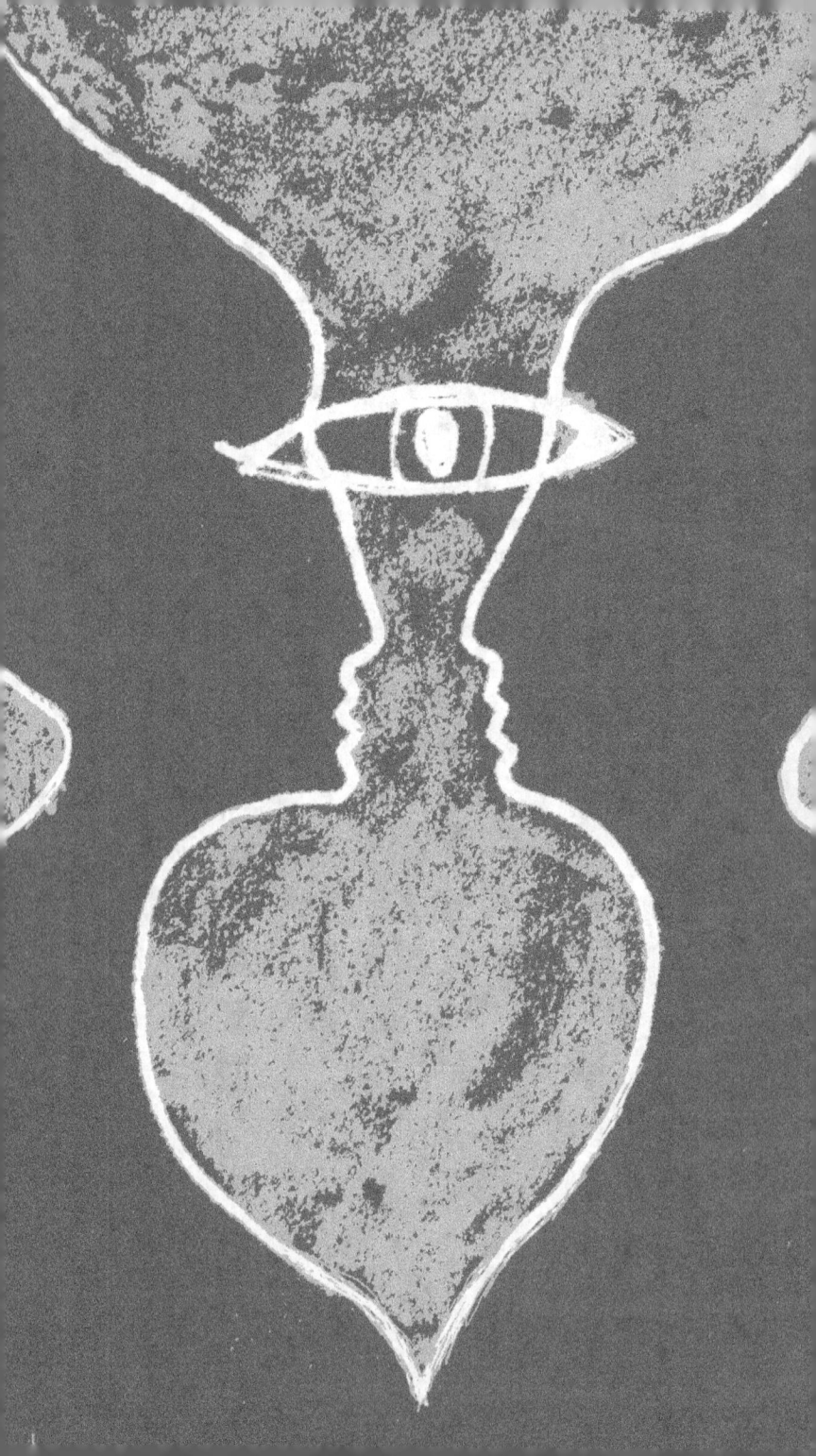

GETTING CLOSER

Devoid of
a certain measure of intensity,
things are becoming
softer, calmer.

Some of our sharp edges
have disappeared,
and pleasantly touched
are we.

SYNTHESIS

One needs to know
how to wait.
Learn it.

Be the one that waits
and the thing waited for–
the subject and object
at the same moment.

There will be no waiting then,
for there will be no other.

Time will cease.
We shall be passing
as a powerful synthesis
of opposites.

MATURED

In the reality that has countless appearances,
it is not easy to reach an opinion –
and is even more difficult to let go of it.

Accumulated opinions
flood our mental space,
hence they burden our moments.

Unconditional acceptance and gratitude
disperse our mental density and
allow an easiness of being to come.

SUPPER

While seated, men are frequently
bothered by their sitting posture,
either in parts of the arm or a left foot toe,
and necessary bodily movements are
performed.

And so, in this room, frequently,
the creaking of the chairs
and a gentle swaying of tables is heard
as the answer to the demands
of the seated bodies,
trying to accommodate
to the energy of time.

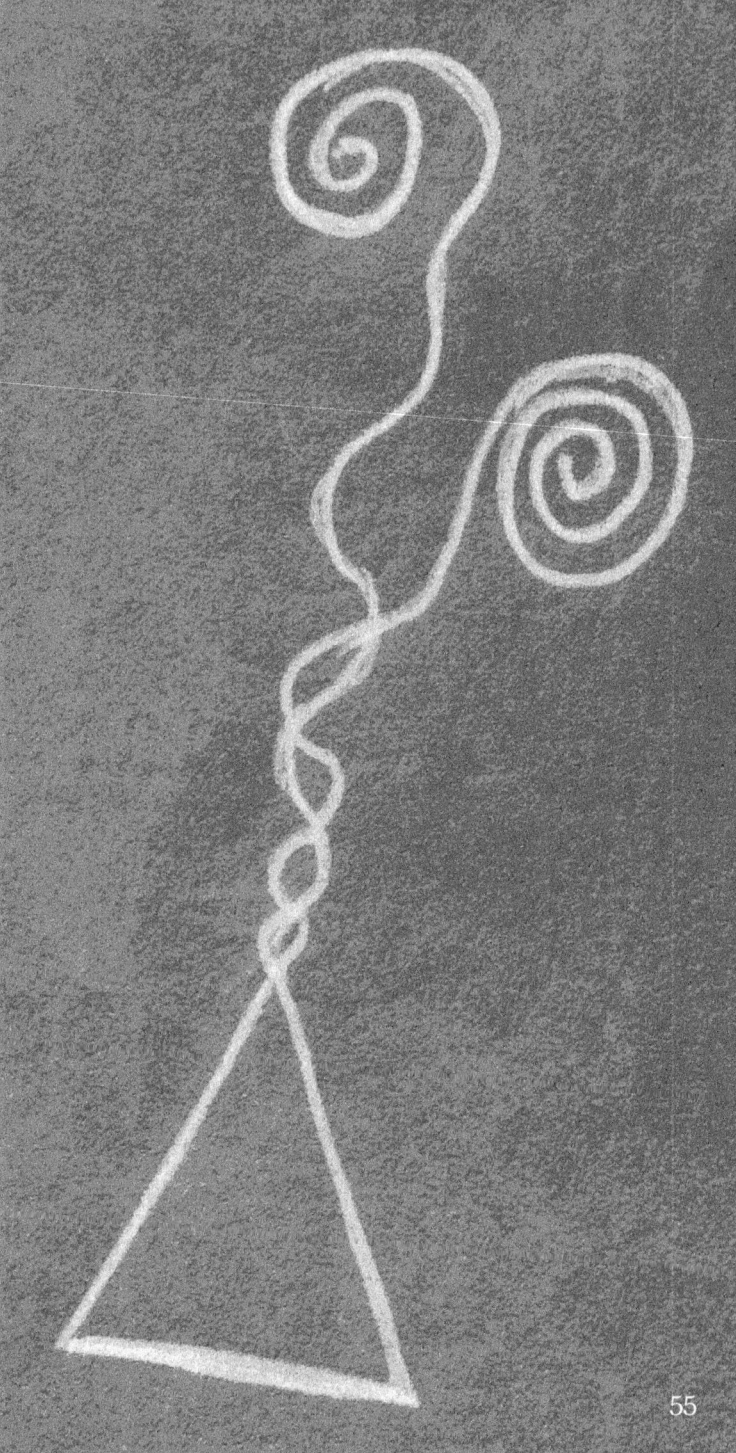

I RECOGNISE

The scent of linden trees
is reigning over the city.

Its intense presence has woken
something primordially mine – a sense
of an unquestionable pleasure of being.

I recognised it
in the way of my breathing
and the way of observing.

Hence in a bundle of people,
in evening whispers, deserted streets,
or in the mundane business
of this big city,
I find the answers
to the questions I don't even ask.

The scent of linden flowers
ushers me into days,
bestowing something greatly needed.

Grateful and quiet I am.

MY SILENCE

Take me on your wings,
my silence!

With you, I wished to fly
away from the kingdom of words –
far away, where the light is golden
and silence is divine.

Take me on your wings,
my silence!

WAKE UP!

BE!

Wake up!

Here are the sounds happening,
here is the song emerging
from the passionate play
of sense with non-sense.

Wake up and enter this moment.
Dress these rhythms
that give and call,
dress your entire desire for beauty
and so enchanted,
BE!

THIS MOMENT

This moment
is the only real one
because it is on.

This moment,
is powerful and endless –
as we are, when belong to it.

By trying to halt it,
we branch off
the Life's strongest flow.

Along the side passages,
the supply with the energy of time
is rather scarce.

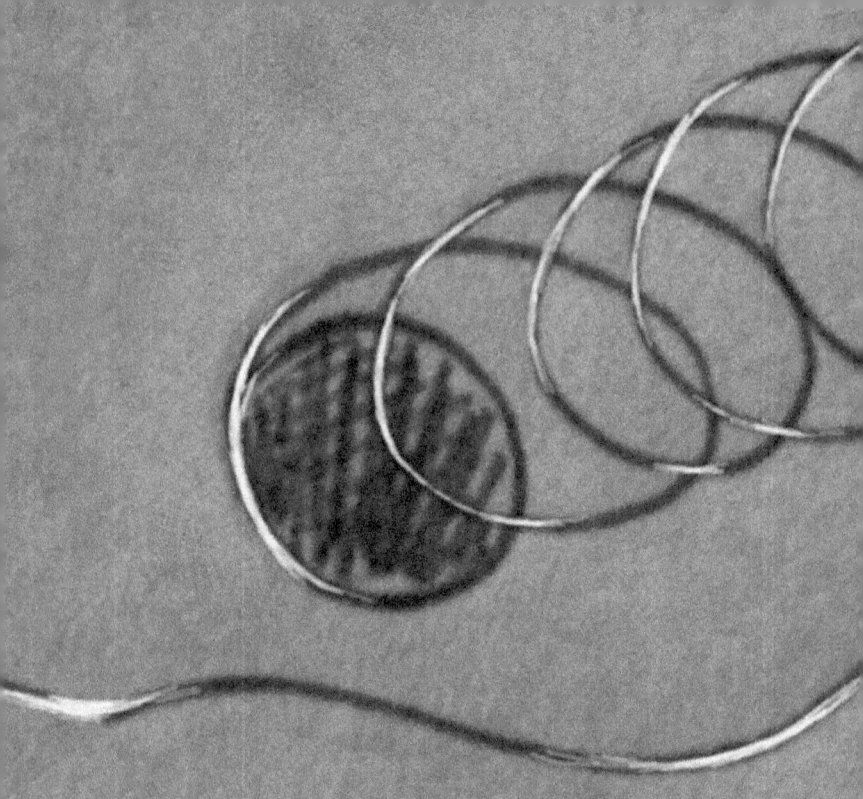

THE REAL DESTINATION

Where am I heading without noticing?

Why to any distant somewhere
when the real destination is within,
in this NOW,
that knots infinities
and speedless flows
knowing all, possessing all.

HERE AND NOW

Stop!
Be for this moment –
it is all there is.

Tomorrow and the past
are mental assets,
a virtual reality.

Missed opportunities,
all unlived, will never be lived
in any future,
for circumstances ceaselessly change.

Stop and enter fully into the NOW
that is rolling along infinities!

Do not hide;
face yourself
and believe!

Fear no failure;
each of them is a step
in a positive direction!

Here and now, on Earth,
there is a cosmic opportunity
to enjoy that you are.

QUESTIONED

Where is my heart
when I use words
and count the reasons?

Where is my divine being
when my terrestrial self
still asks
"WHY"?

RELIABLE COMPANION

My dear mind,
for how long more
would you try to understand
that which heart naturally knows?

You would not be mind
if you would not stick to the rational,
and get serious about this question.

Heart is here to collaborate with you.
As one wisdom, you can easier navigate
through the ocean of breath.

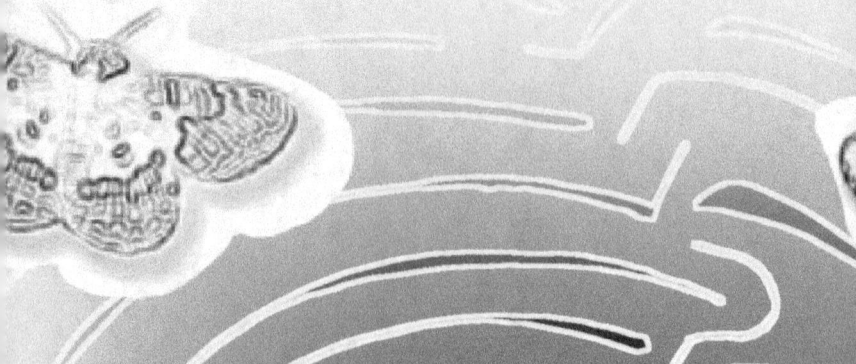

CHOICELESS

I cannot lock you in,
my heart,
so that you don't long
and don't want.

You are free to expand,
even though
you are looking for intimacy
and feed it.

Acceptance is your way,
and closeness its manifestation;
closeness – as a pure joy.

ENCOURAGEMENT

River of life is turbulent,
wind is occasionally strong.

Grow stronger, my heart!
The ocean of neutral consciousness
is faraway
yet –
ready for you.

THERE IS A SEA

The estuary is common
to all nightmares and pains.

We flow to where the river,
empowered, loses itself.

Into the secret of the sea,
in its confined infinity, we hurry;
we – the cosmic seeds planted on Earth.

And do not catch butterflies along the way!

O, ENDLESSNESS!

1. RETURNING TO YOU

O, Endlessness inside me,
here I am, coming to you
after years of absence.
I am bringing to you all my tears
which fed my non-sleep.

O, Endlessness inside me,
I remember you now,
when a word is painfully misused,
when a smile disappears,
uncontinued on others' lips,
when there is no answer
for longings which hurt.

O, Endlessness inside me,
I am certain now
that you are everything I ever had,
that I am yours since you've conceived me
and that, in your dimension only
I exist fully.

2. FORGIVE ME.

O, Endlessness inside me,
my path and my shelter!

Forgive all my wanderings,
my expectation of you from others.

Understand my fruitless curiosities –
in search for myself,
they were taking me
to faces and hearts of the strangers.

I let them enchant me
with their words and smiles
while I looked for you
in their eyes,
and from their fingers
expected your touch.

I am exhausted by my dependence on events,
I am worn out by my expectations.
I do not want to depend on them,
I do not want to depend at all.

3. ACCEPT ME

O, Endlessness inside me,
every window of my soul
is opening to you
and my inner fires are lit again.

Finally, I am neglecting much of trivia
and climbing to you,
to present to you what only stayed mine
– myself alone,
with each breath committed to you.

Accept me imperfect.
Accept me saturated with pain.

4. THANK YOU

O, Endlessness inside me,
long ago it was when I discovered you,
when we belonged to each other.
Why did I ever forget you,
investing myself
into numerous expectations?

I thank you, Endlessness inside me,
for sending messages to me
from numberless places,
for sending people
and orchestrating events
to entice me back to you, to me.

The game of navigation
has lasted too long.
Now you are here,
tangibly inside me,
O, Endlessness.

5. TEACH ME

Love me, Endlessness inside me!
Love me even for those
who refused to love me.

Cherish me inside yourself.
(If necessary, I will be your secret.)

Teach me
that I do not need to remember
those bitter, convincing,
non-findings.

Teach me
to be serene even more;
teach me
to love unconditionally.

Convince me
that I already have all I need.

Teach me not to question;
teach me not to wish;
Teach me infinite patience.

Take me to the Absolute Time
O, Endlessness inside me.

6. WAS WORTH IT

O, Endlessness inside me,
still everything that happened was worth it
because everything that was seemingly
taking me away from you,
in actuality was directing me to you, to me.

I thank you for the reasons
of all my tears on this road –
their river has brought me to you.

O, Endlessness inside me,
I understand now that you have observed my path,
letting me rediscover you
in an inevitable way and moment.

Now, the walk is becoming easier
since the path is shining with lights
of my increased awareness.

PRAYER

O my words,
exhausted now,
let me envelop you in silence
while you recover.

ONLY
LOVE
CAN
ENDURE
THIS
SILENCE

RUSSIAN CHIMES

PRESENT AND ABSENT

A calm river is glittering in the sun.
Boats are asleep, church domes smiling.
Clouds are bowing down
before the sight of this beauty.

In a moment I might even start flying.
Joy is spreading.
I am blending into the scenery.

Russia, I have come to you,
but – I am disappearing.

CALL

What is that calling me alone
through this sound of Russian bells?

Heavens! Worlds!
– I can hear you arriving to this moment
and staying here,
moored by the fibres of tranquillity.

With my eyes open wide
I look up.
Still here, but where am I?

Bells – the calling sound
of timelessness!

I shall run to it!

ON THE BOAT

I am sitting on the river
in a small boat, lazy to move
through the glowing eternity
spread over the calm water.

Church domes on the banks are soundless
yet eloquent on their rich past.

Silence is everywhere
coming from the water,
from mysterious distances.

How can one grasp
this melancholic beauty that is growing,
the time which has it
and this me –
sitting on a forgotten river
of the Milky Way galaxy.

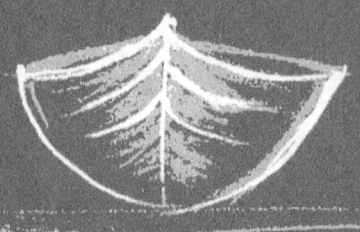

RUSSIAN CHIMES

While the Russian chimes cry,
the aeons of silence
dismally shed their colours.

UKRAINE

Birds are rising in the fields,
together with the sounds of blue silence.

Yet another eternity
to be comprehended!

INEVITABILITY

I want this moment to be named.

The train has departed from St. Petersburg:
a monotonous sound continues,
a display of birch woods in both windows
goes on.

Some people have stayed,
because some have left.
It is an inevitability,
the same as the clattering of this train.

New feelings, with a fresh outlook on reality,
and new harmonies are growing inside of me.

RUSSIA

Once upon a time
there was a country,
far off and sad
– Russia.

In its grandness,
lost somewhere.

In eternity
preserved somewhere!

A POSTERIORI

After Russia,
I feel as if a sea has carried me for days
and rocked me
with its most beautiful movements,
then left me on its shore
giving me something precious
– to carry in my smile, and share.

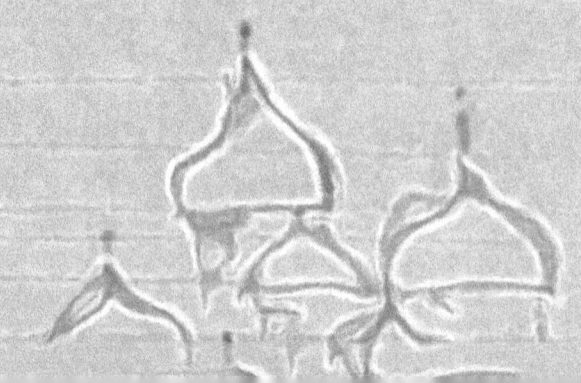

REPLICA

Bells,
here, by these thoughts,
transfixed
into a late summer afternoon.

Bells,
like a scent,
like a chimera.

Bells,
like a fickle light
or a colour desired.

Bells,
sonorously resonant
— as memories.

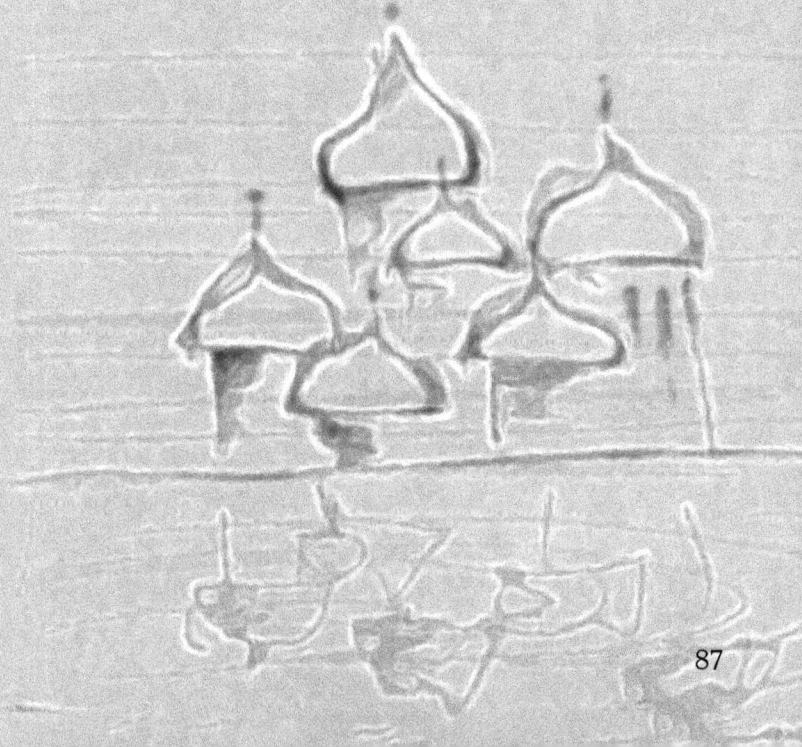

I AM DISAPPEARING KNOWING NOT WHERE YOU ARE

THE END OF SUMMER

With the childhood on my fingertips,
a summer has gone
and you on its waves.

You wanted me not to have you
so you didn't have me either.

There was a pain.

I understand –
as the summer had to pass,
I had to grow.

I SHALL TELL YOU

I am that which flows,
always something new.

COMES YOUR NON-COMING

Never would you come.
I know.
I am ready for it.

So, don't come.
That non-coming
will complete the meaning
of your appearance on my path
and give me more –
teaching me more
about me.

And really, do not come!
Stay where the others are
who got lost in their desire
or non-desire to approach me.

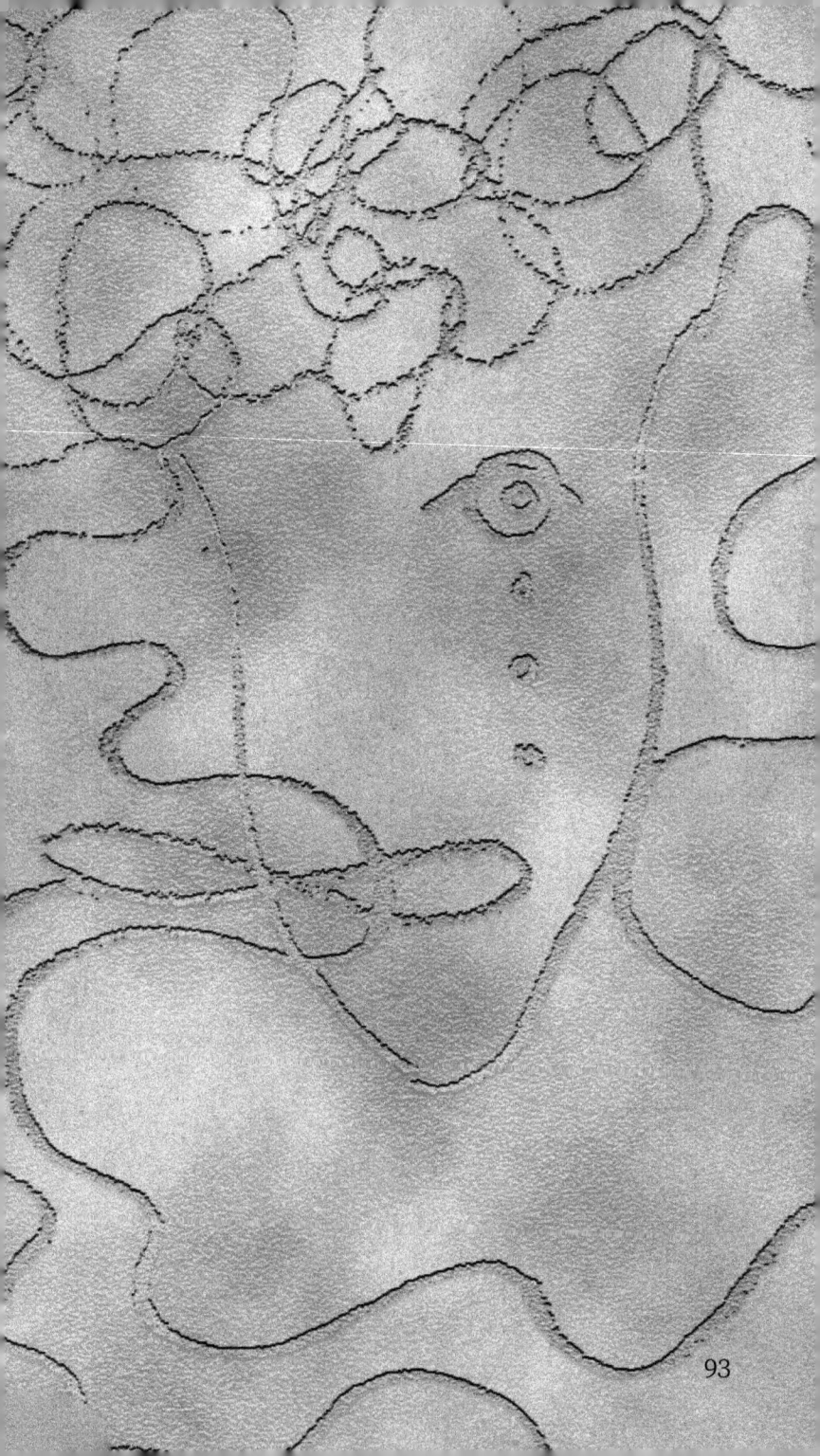

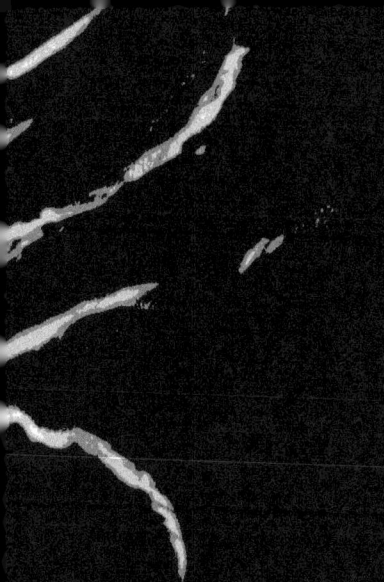

PAIN

The trees beside me
became even more silent
and greener in surprise.

The river flew
by not accepting me
in its eternity.

And the sky darkened
upon my cry.

Forgive me,
but you are the reason
for my bewilderment.

I reject this hour.
The screams of non-sleeps
tear me apart,
feeding on white tears.

LONGING

And nothing is here
in this rain and night.
Only the lost are calling
one another.

You are not here.
My thoughts are leaving me
while I am facing the pain,
trying to free myself from it.

Do you exist – as the one
my longing conjures up –
or this yearning
is just tirelessly idealising?

COME

My gates are open
and guards are
not there any longer.

Couldn't you feel
this shear magnitude
of my readiness
and this desire.

Come!

INNER FIRE

This longing for you
never ends, but grows stronger.
I am burning.
The fierce magnitude of that fire
reaches my essence.

What a volcano I am,
hidden in this seemingly
quiet body and mind.

Is there more I could ever wish for?

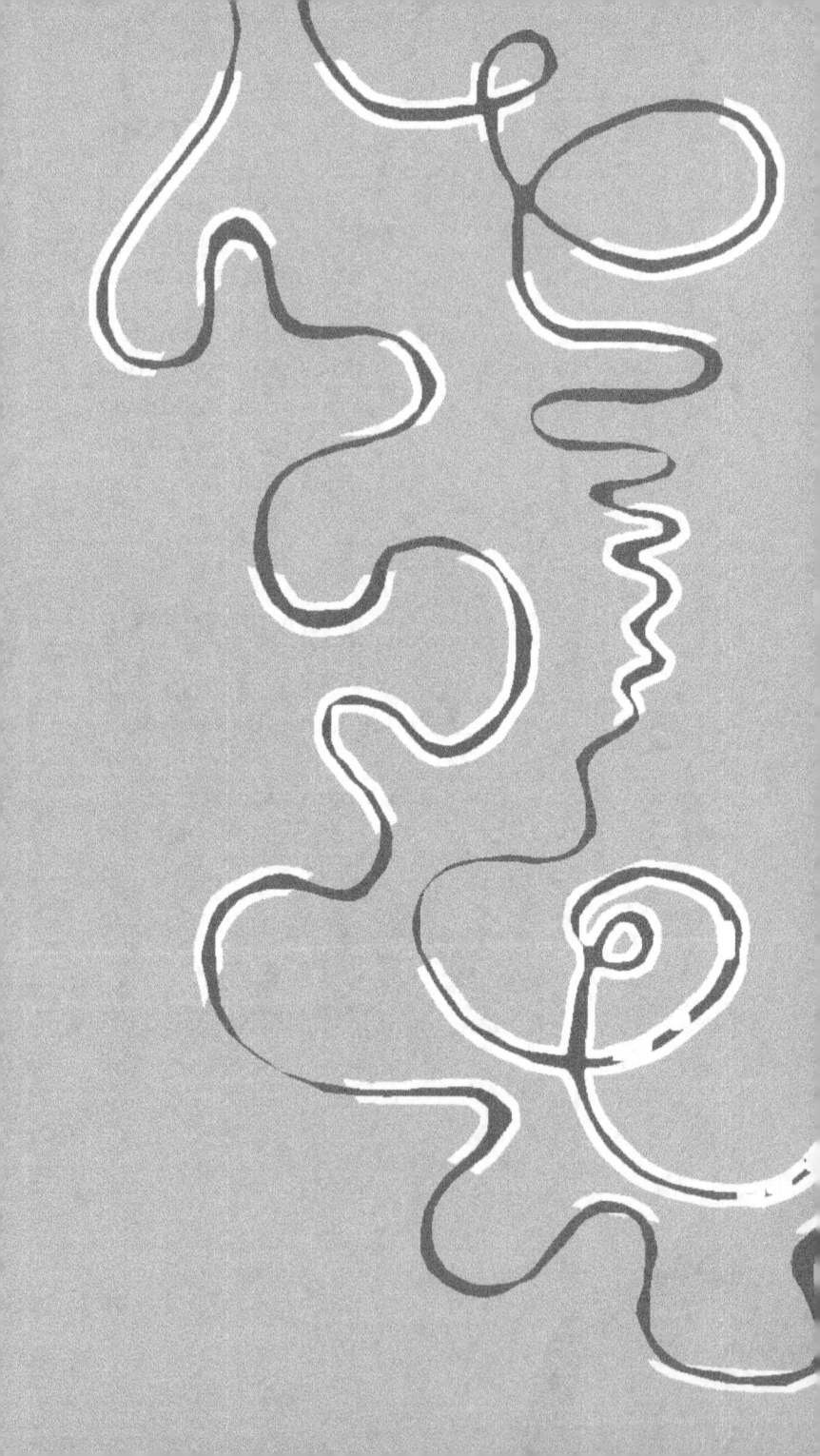

SPARKLES

Let us dive
inside one another,
till we no longer
can know the selves,
till only ecstasy remains
as yet another
sparkle
of the heavens.

WHIRLPOOL

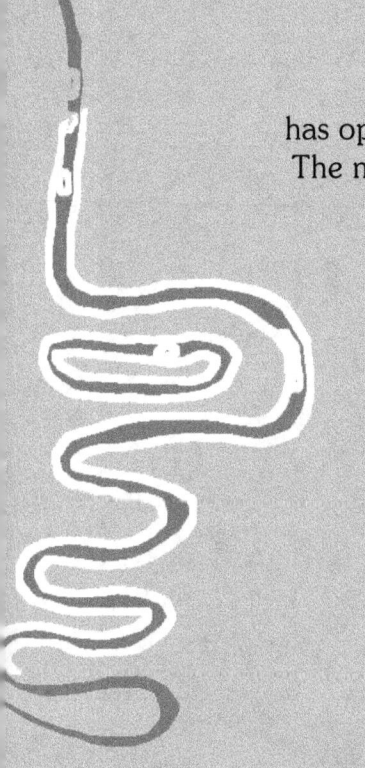

Flows the river
forgetting about me.

Longing for you
has opened a whirlpool in my heart.
The moments of solitude are heavy,
thinking of you hurts.

I need a run in the fields
and a talk with the forest.

Something of me
ought to be torn apart
and left to this endless day.

A master of change
in each instant,
a river could teach me
the art of letting go.

I need a run in the fields
and a talk with the river.

BEING

It is all a long path of footsteps.
Our solitude is the same
and we copy its letters.
We face the same wall.

Must I write to you,
who I will not see
nor touch,
someone I dream of?

You can keep your distance
as far as the Moon or Cassiopeia
and not see me,
nor understand me,
you can forget my tiresomeness
and the round rambling,
throw me into the Styx
and go away.
You can do it all.

Silent,
I will be here,
in my eyes
and my fingers.

YOU

Rumble the inaudible sounds
of my being.

I do not know how nor why
but I need you.

I confess,
your passing by makes me restless,
the failure to have you and this pain.
Therefore I wish not to long for you this much.

You and I!
How eternal,
how terrestrially impossible
this union sounds!

You…
may I, at least, dream of you?

HELPLESS

Oh, my fool,
how long will this game go on?
You shuffled a purpose of mine,
poked a thousand cells,
moved into a beginning of mine.

You fill me and you win me over,
day in and day out
– though you are not here.
Not even my tears can call you in.

I have been asking the dark
and the snow about you.

I am waiting.
What am I to do?

A WISH

You are only a maybe,
yet a pain and a shiver
– a convincing chimera of mine.

I am renewing you
with what was initiated through you,
and while forgetting to reason
I want you more.

The night is quiet,
its silence is heavy –
suffocating me with Everything
that without you is called Nothing.

Forgetting to reason,
I want you more.

Who is stronger:
my mind or my heart?

Would I ever know?

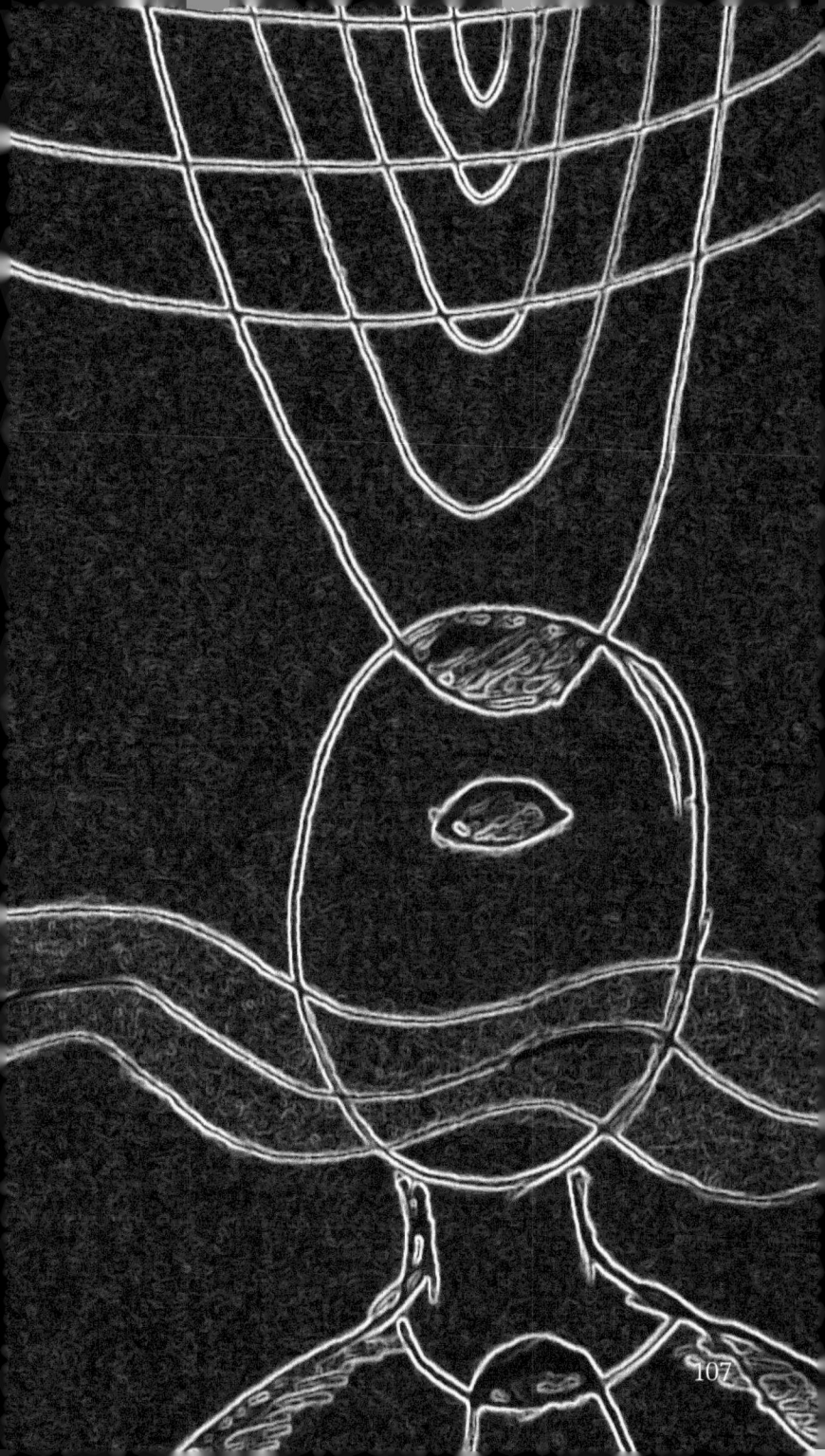

DAWN

Only the night remained with me
and we are dying together
to the joy of wasted light
riding from the East,
powerful but insignificant
because I shall be no more.

The brook, tomorrow, the wounds
– do not hurt me any more,
only the silence, memories
and a dream.

I am disappearing
knowing not where you are.

PHOENIX

Longing conceives you
and maintains you.

Longing uses you
and it wears you out.

Where do you exist?

THE REAL

Meeting with you was not virtual.
I know, it was real.

I know it from the speed of my breathing,
I know it from the joy of my thinking.

I have not seen you since,
nor have I touched you,
but you have been mine
as much as I wanted.

Meeting with you
was not my chimera.

It became even more real
when you vanished.

With you, I disappeared too
yet out of pain was born again:
stronger, different –
richer for a new ascension
earned by each of my cells.

SONG OF DEAD BIRDS

Strengthened by desire to be,
words escaped my control and,
like birds freed from a cage,
flew towards you.

Surprised with the energy of that multitude
and feared,
you turned them
into a flock of dead fliers.

When, if ever, you open your soul
and you hear odd sounds,
that will be my pain
changed into songs
in the beaks of dead birds
wandering through time.

DEAD GAME

Close your box of words
and stop playing with them.

Their suddenly changed direction
found me unprepared
and killed silently.

Now I watch my deadness
in every movement I make.

Dead me and distant you –
isn't it too big a price
for our incompatibility,
or for the suitability
too weak to realise itself.

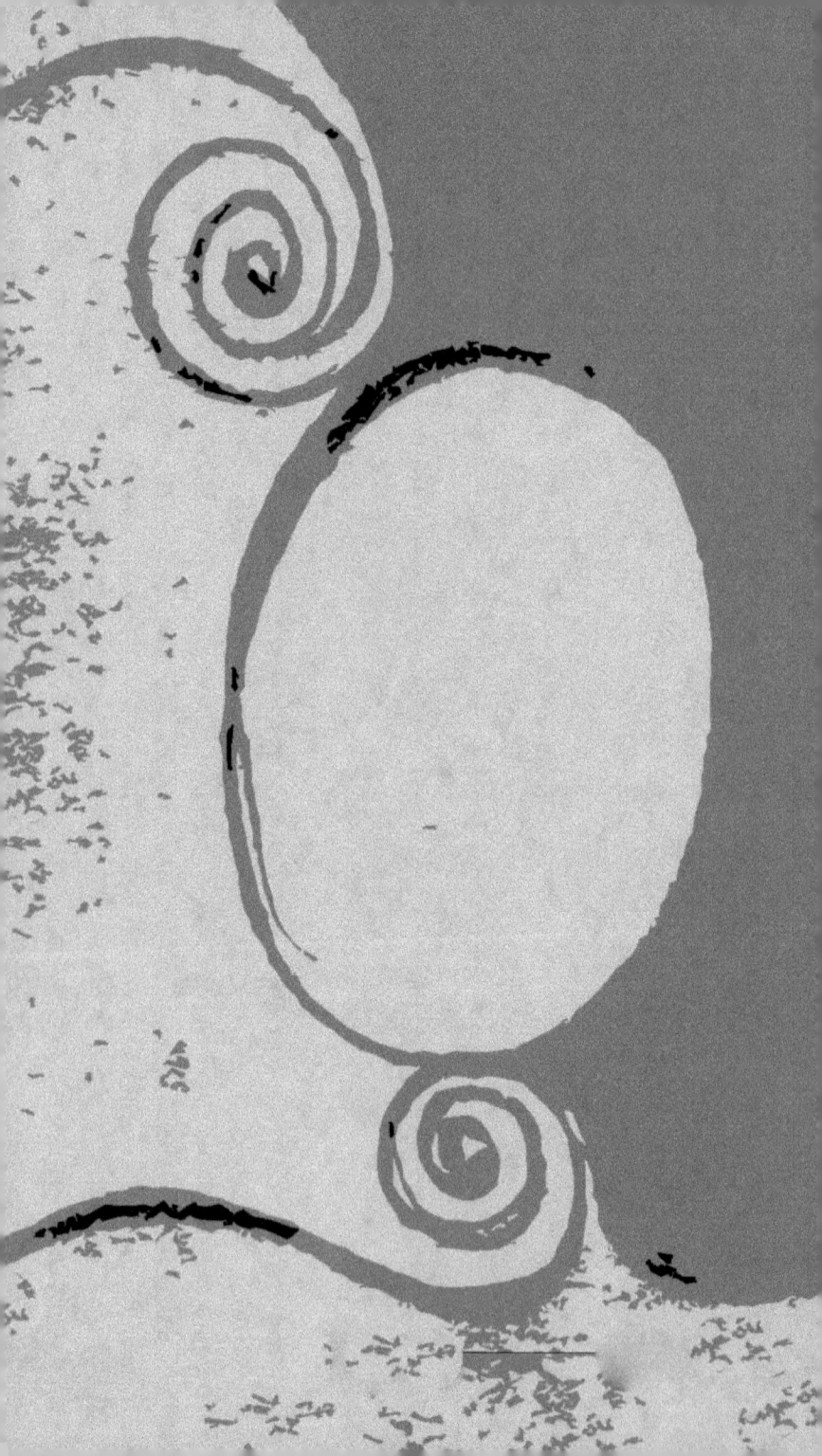

BEST VIEW

Take your promises with you
to happen somewhere else.
Please, go with it
and forget that ever
you walked into my world.

Do go far,
where my thoughts
cannot reach you.

I will stay here,
here where I have to be –
in myself.

From that place, the view is best
and there everything already exists –
even you, better and more real.

REALISATION

From me to you – a three days' walk.
How this monumental incompatibility
resulted in an attraction?

You do not fit into my path.
I am so clear of it,
Clear to the core.

I do not want,
I do not expect (anymore).

I have.

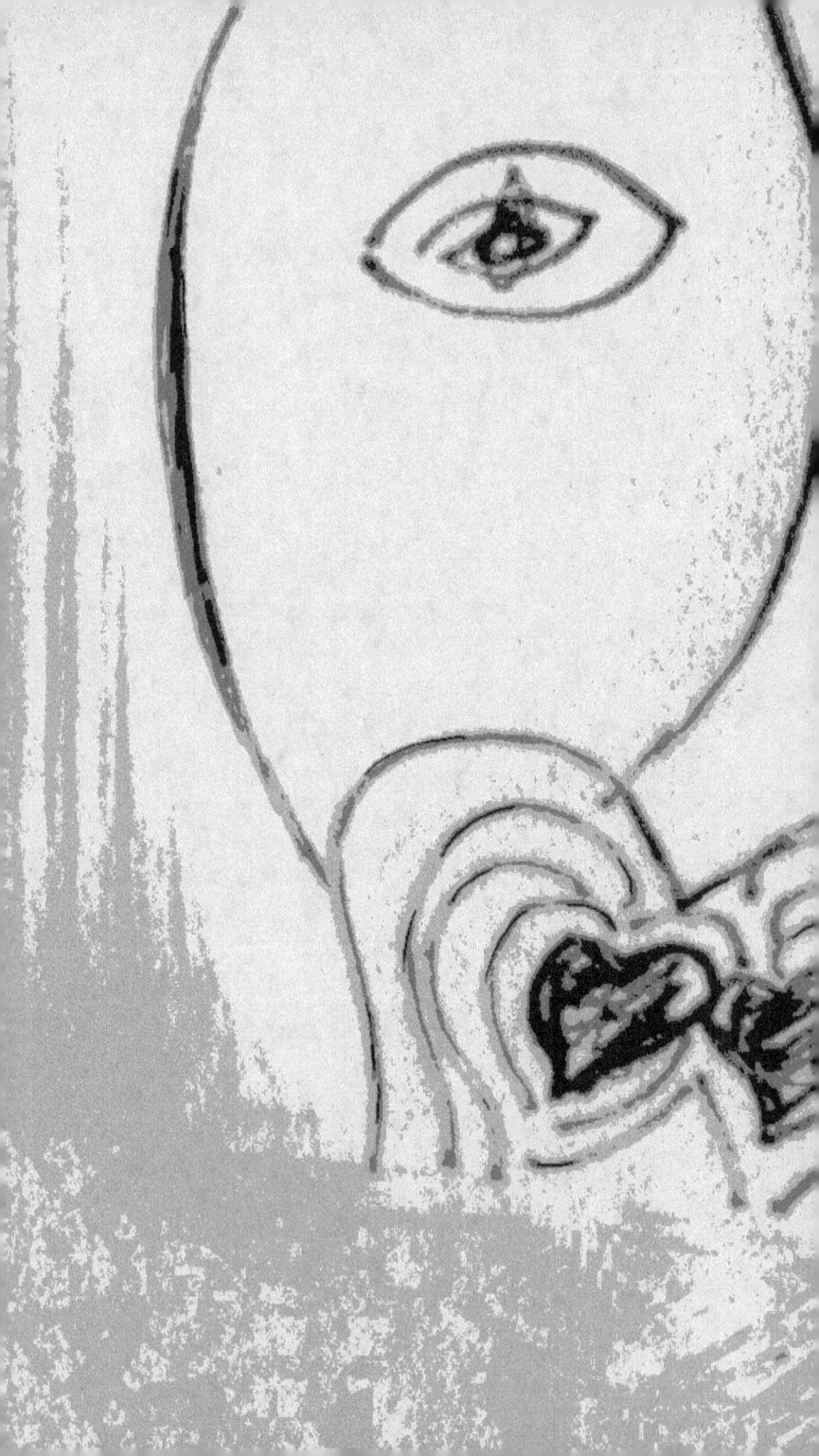

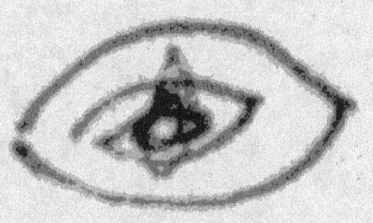

EVENTUALLY

I am looking at you gone
and feel that you are already back,
that you are inside me –
intending nowhere to go.

I am looking at you gone
and embracing your body
grown into mine.

I am looking at you gone
while listening to you present.

Eventually, I don't know
where you are anymore.

Eventually, I don't know
where I am anymore.

Do I need to know?

NIGHT VISIT

Just when I believed I wished you no longer,
stronger than dream, a desire for you
wakes me up
bringing you into my body.

Master of all my cells,
I am yours again!

I feel it while,
without voice and shapeless,
you are flooding me
in the dark silence of this night,
so eternity alike.

And, it hurts nicely.

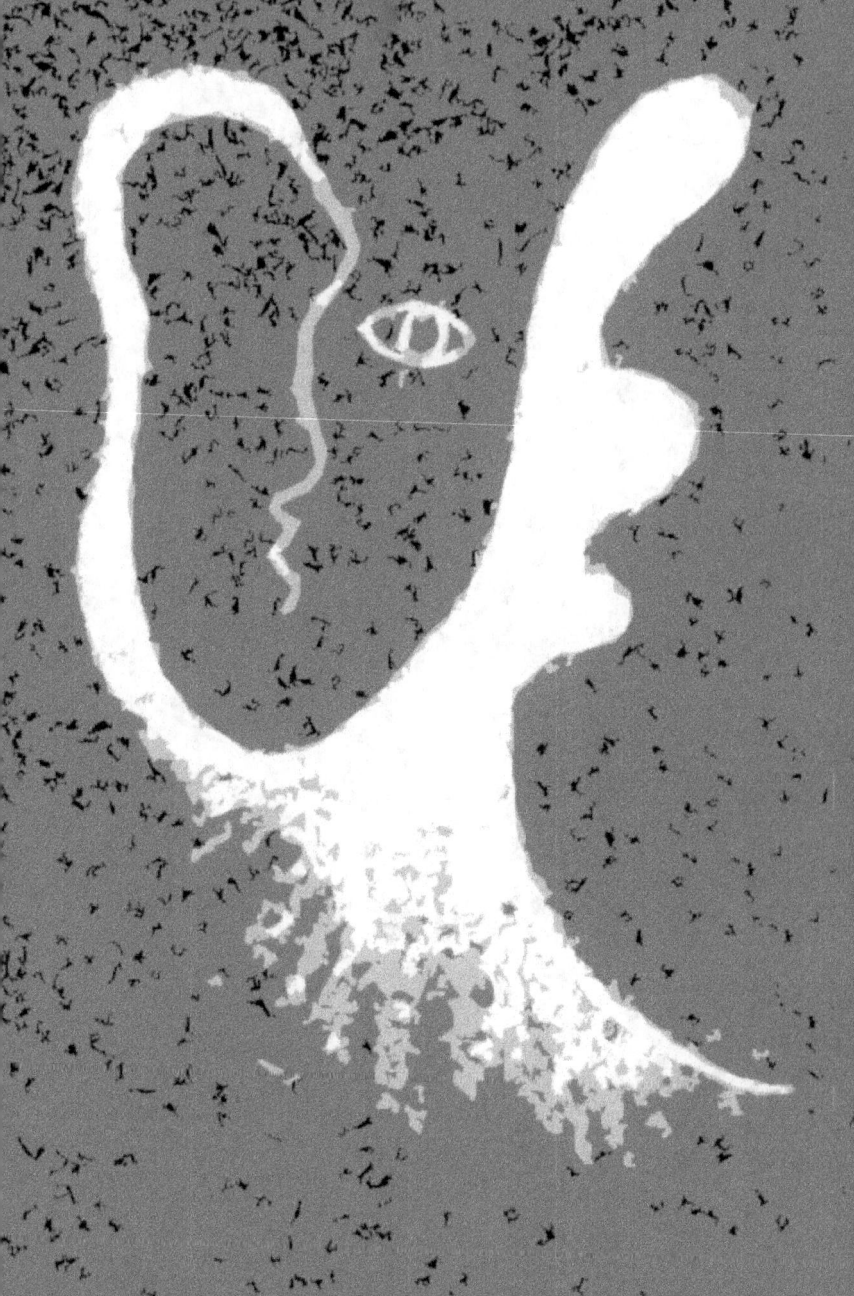

YOU ARE ME

It is now late for you to leave.

You are already in, you are me.

And there is even no way
for you to disappear
– every cell of mine
has processed you,
so you are already in,
you are me.

Knowing this or not,
you are already in,
you are me.

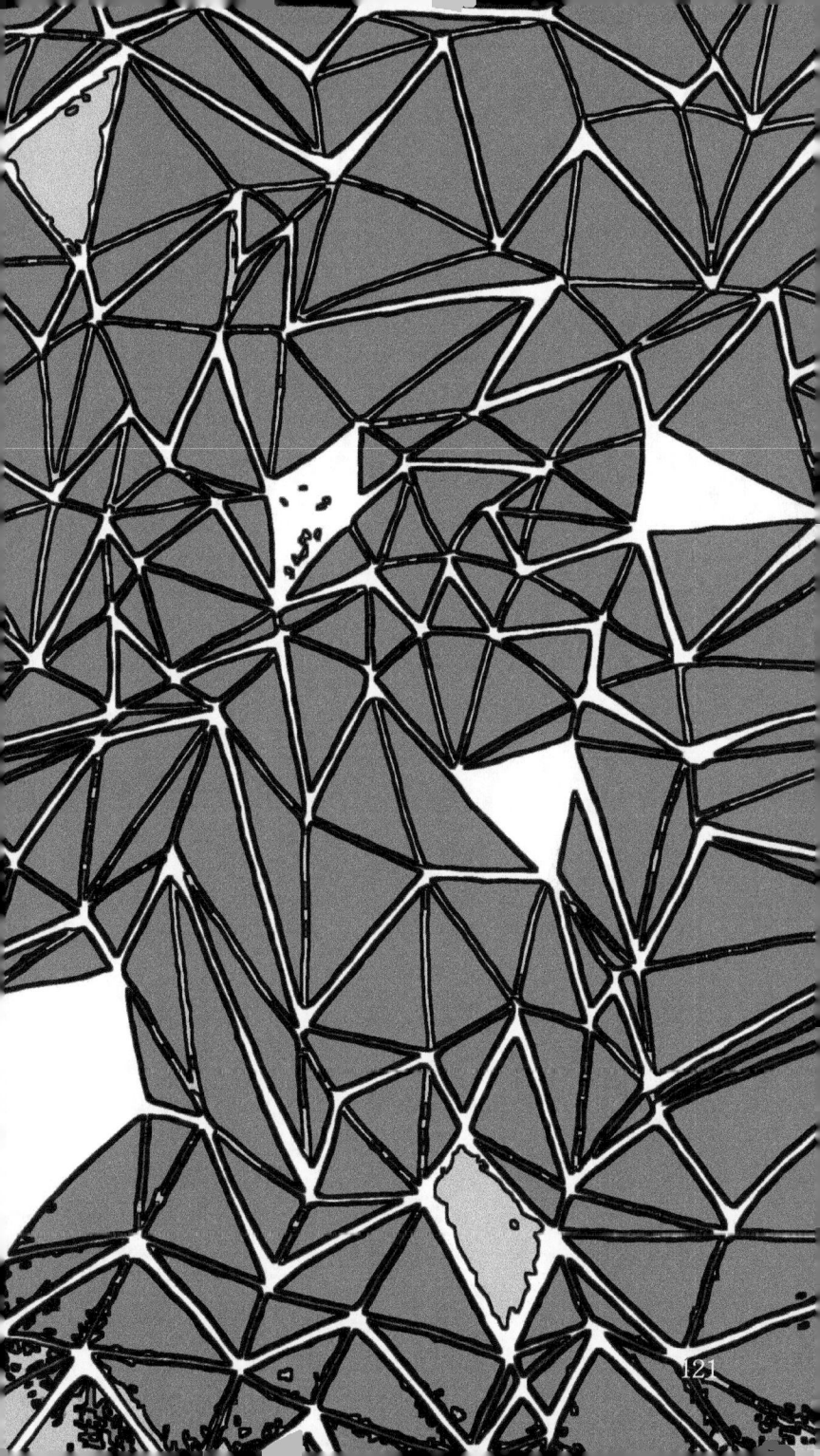

DEAR LORD ...

WHAT ELSE CAN I DO

Dear Lord,
I have nowhere to go,
but to explore this self
within Your realness;
and nothing to do
but express my gratitude
for this opportunity.

I know, You have been waiting for
this threshold of my evolution
for aeons already.

You would be prepared to wait even longer
but I would not.

I crave my constant awareness about You.

YOUR PRESENCE

Dear Lord,
only now do I recognise
Your sweet presence within –
Your growing lights
that feed me,
and guide me,
towards my cosmic potential.

TOUCH

While I was dreaming about You,
Dear Lord,
You stretched Your hand
through that dream
and touched me.

From that touch
I remembered me,
I remembered You,
and ascended
into a divine bliss.

I cherish that vibration
and let it reinforce me,
on this one-way walk
that loops back into itself,
into its own beginning.

WAKING UP

We have never been apart –
it only was my years-long sleep
that maintained that illusion.

With being asleep is over
since my growing awareness about You
wakes me up more, in each moment.

I understand now –
You can only be away from me
for as long as my forgetting myself lasts!

ESSENCE KNOWING

I have You in my heart,
I have You in my flesh, bones,
in the wholeness of my energies.

You are in the very essence
of my knowing of this.

Still, where does this
insatiable longings come from
when we are already One,
Dear Lord?

GETTING CLOSER

Every time I find You within,
You connect me with beyondness,
and by feeding
the metaphysical certainty of my being
You offer a new meaning
to my terrestrial presence.

Hence, I am learning
to make myself more available to us,
Dear Lord.

The closer we become,
The less bearable it is
to live unaware of You –
even for a split second.

SACRED PLACE

There is a place
in my heart
where I easily find You,
Dear Lord –
should humbleness
bring me there.

You welcome that reunion
with the smiling warmth
of Your realness.

In such a state of nested infinities
boundaries disappear;
bliss flows through avenues of awareness
and individuality loses its meaning,
Dear Lord.

COSMIC HOMELAND

"You are coming home, My child.

I observe your love guiding you.
I see your obstacles and doubts.
I understand your pain and fears,
and salute your perseverance and faith.

I am proud of you, My dear children,
yet cannot show you all My love
since you will not grow
and obey Me anymore,
but stay forever where you are.

However, in the shiny chambers of your heart,
within My Heart, I am waiting for you.

Intellect only, will never elevate you enough.
If you couple it with the logic of heart,
you will unlock the gates of My universes."

PROGRAMME

"In the form of other faces and beings,
it has always been Me
who wanted to come closer to you,
so that you come closer
to your real self – to Me.

All your ups and downs were the peculiar rocking
that I do to My Children to wake them up.

They are My Programme prepared to shift you
into the vibrational level of your essence –
of My Essence."

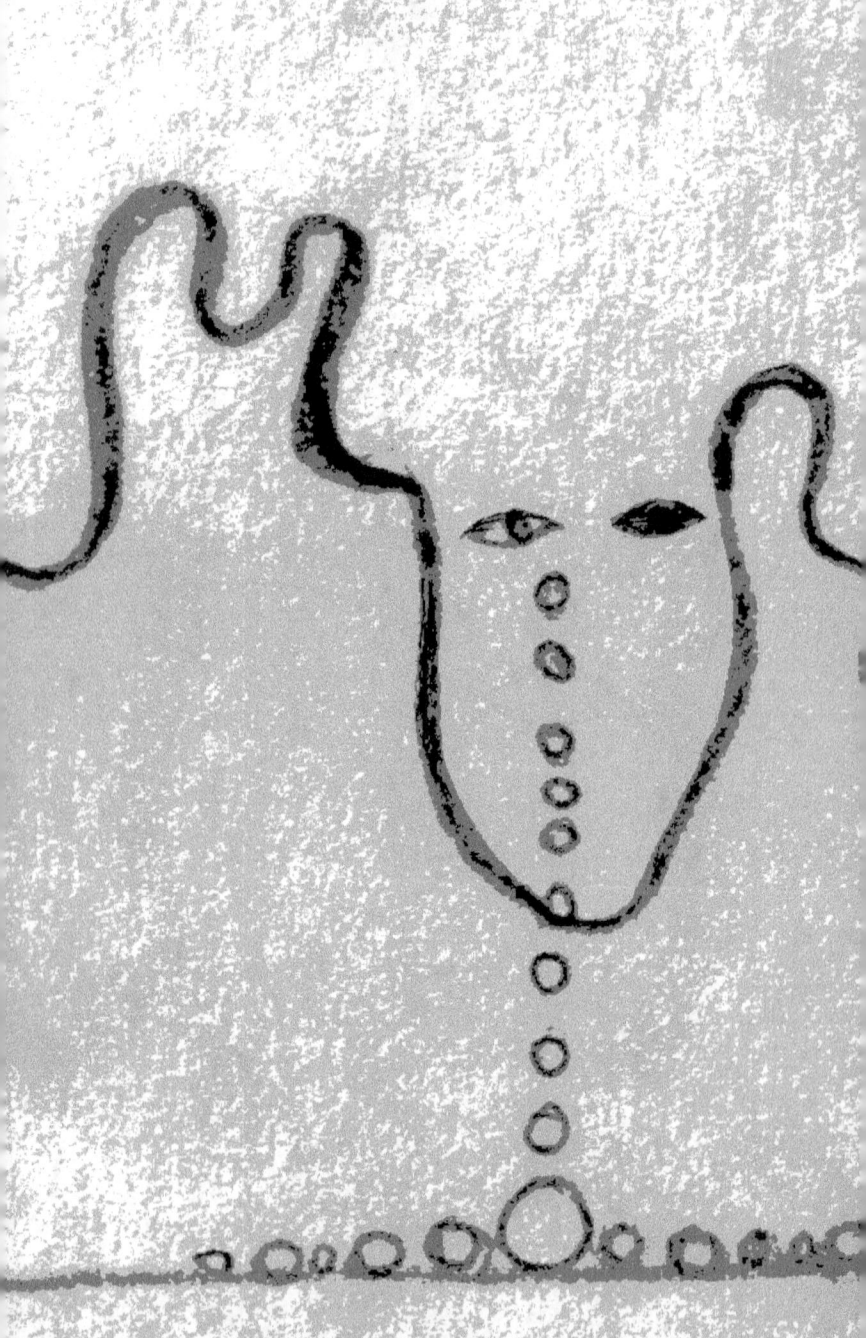

TEARS

"Through all your pain
I was with you,
holding you and lifting you up.

I am healing your wounds
by making you experience new ones,
until you stop noticing them,
until you realise
that pain is an experience
necessary at particular level of consciousness.

When you cry,
I let My sorrow pour out through your tears
to cleanse My Creation."

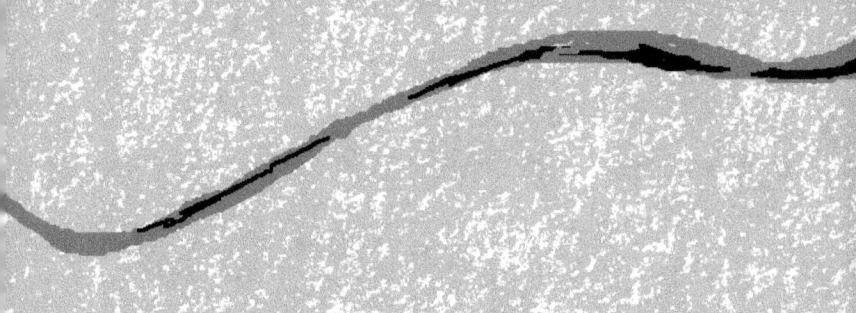

DIRECT EXPERIENCE

What colour is your magic,
Dear Lord?
You do not need to tell me,
just paint it on me,
inside me,
around me,
around the world and stars.

"I've already done that" –
I hear You saying.
But, what colour is it? –
keeps asking Your
child-like Earthly aspect.

"It is a secret, it is My secret."

Thank You Lord,
for reminding me that
some secrets will remain secrets.

When we learn to observe,
answers come through direct experiences
and we know that we know.

INSPIRATOR

O, my Owner, my Master
within the Infinite Void,
please, can You write to me
as I write to You.

"It has always been
this fusion of ours
that moves your hand."
– I hear You saying.

"It is the inspirational energy
of Oneness
that does it,
in longing to translate
the Divine into
the comprehensible."

O, my Owner,
my Master.

ALL OF ALL

Love, love, love…
what is it,
Dear Lord?

"It is a cosmic glue
that maintains My entirety.

Dear Child,
it is you,
it is Me,
it is only One of US."

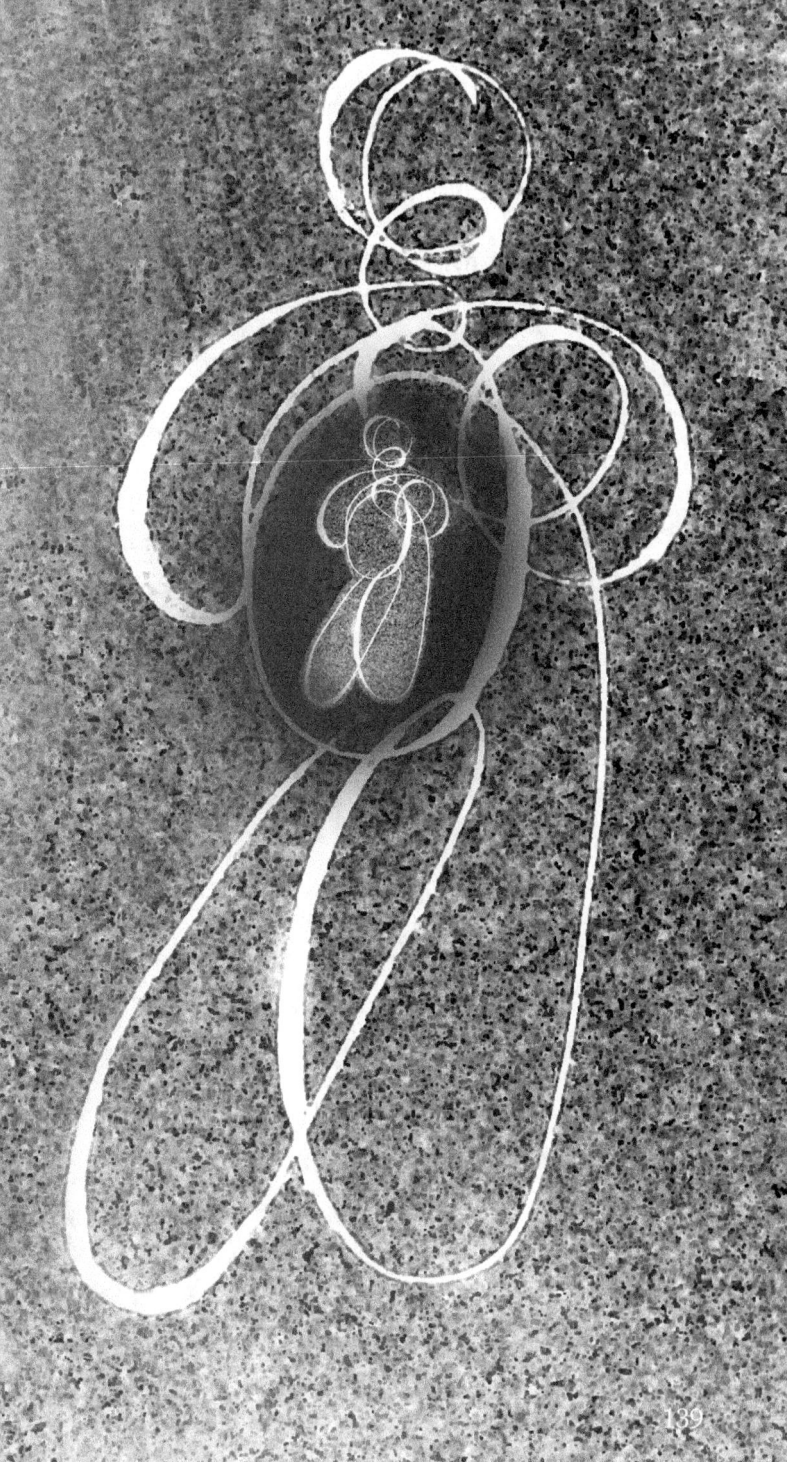

REMIND ME

Colour me
with all Your sounds,
show to me
what I even do not want to see,
take me into the unknown!

Be good,
be naughty through me –
yet, keep reminding me
of my godliness,
Dear Lord!

INNER SMILE

Through the tranquillity
of cosmic silences,
our loves were calling one another.

In the realm of matter,
our loves have met one another.

My inner smile tells it all.

MAGICIAN

You shine through stars,
smile through flowers
sing through birds and
souls in love –
You are all these
and You are mine!

I feel You within and observe You
ordering my energies
through Your supreme ordinances,
Dear Lord.

Even though You are the entire vastness,
of everything there is,
all shapes and colours,
You manage to stay unreachable.

What a magician You are!

COMMON NAME

I know You are
for I know I am,
Dear Lord.

The more I know of who I am
the more I know of You.

Awareness
is our common field.

"I AM"
is our common name.

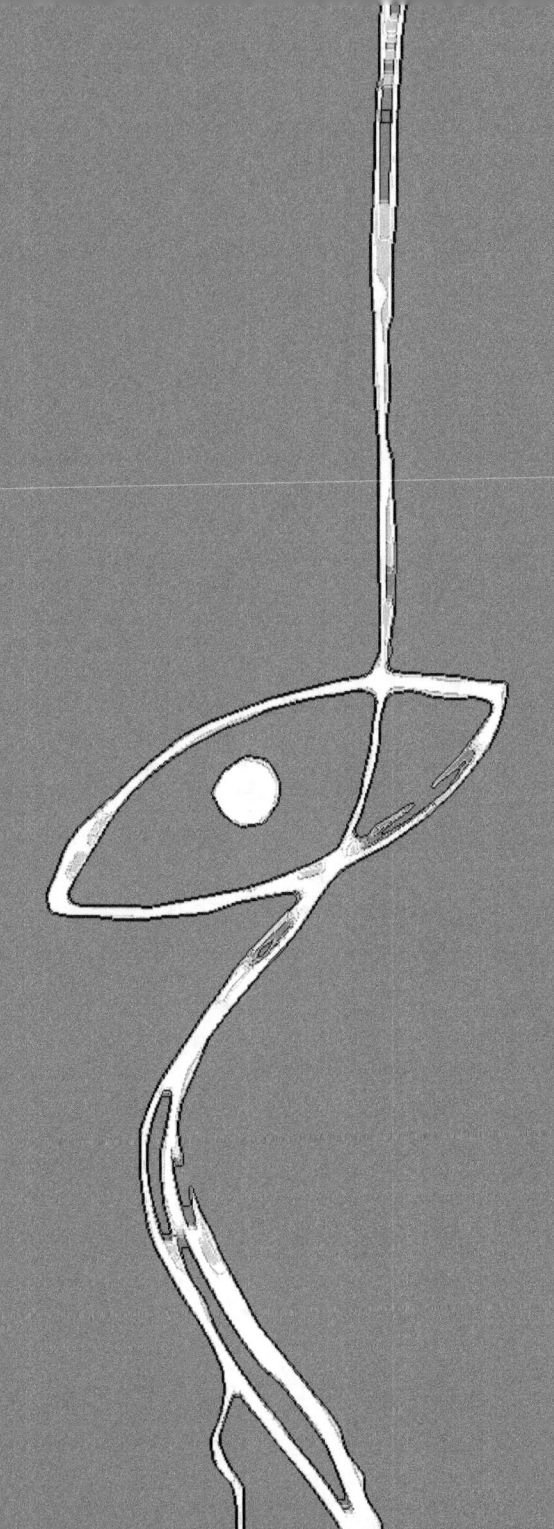

143

APPROACHING

I see You
behind every cause,
Dear Lord,
hence I am losing
my questions.

I work on building my strengths
in order to come closer to You
and survive
– reaching immortality.

LESSONS

You teach me the power of silence,
You teach me to find You within.

You teach me to understand *I AM*.

Knowing me better than I do,
You open new dimensions to me
– in accord with Your Orders
and my capacity.

You taught me to walk, to run, to talk.
One day You will teach me to fly.

UNIQUENESS

It does not matter, Dear Lord,
in how many aspects You exist.

There will always be a frequency
in which You are just for me
and I am just for You.

Thank You,
for supplying me with life force
through that sacred connection.

This is what each human can say.

LIFE-GIVER

Merely thinking of You,
Dear Lord,
awakens some sleeping aspects
of myself.

Without this divine awareness,
all terrestrial views
would perpetually maintain their stances,
incapable of transcending their own level.

Just being aware of You,
enables me to live and love
deeper.

How life-giving You are,
Dear Lord.

WHAT AND WHERE

Sometimes,
Dear Lord,
this body,
this heart,
and mind,
even this world,
seem not enough.

Where am I to be,
to embrace you fully?

And why do I hurry?
Where?
Have we not already met,
Dear Lord?

SOVEREIGN

I know, Dear Lord,
that all is good,
well – even perfect and that,
according to Your Programmes,
everything goes through necessary phases
evolving to their higher forms.

Thus, my lack of interest
to control or insist,
is noticeably growing.

I am giving up MY ways
while gradually transferring
"my" will to You
– to the immaculate interplay
of Your orders.

Finally,
conscious of the universal laws,
I bow before their primacy
and before Your Sovereignty.

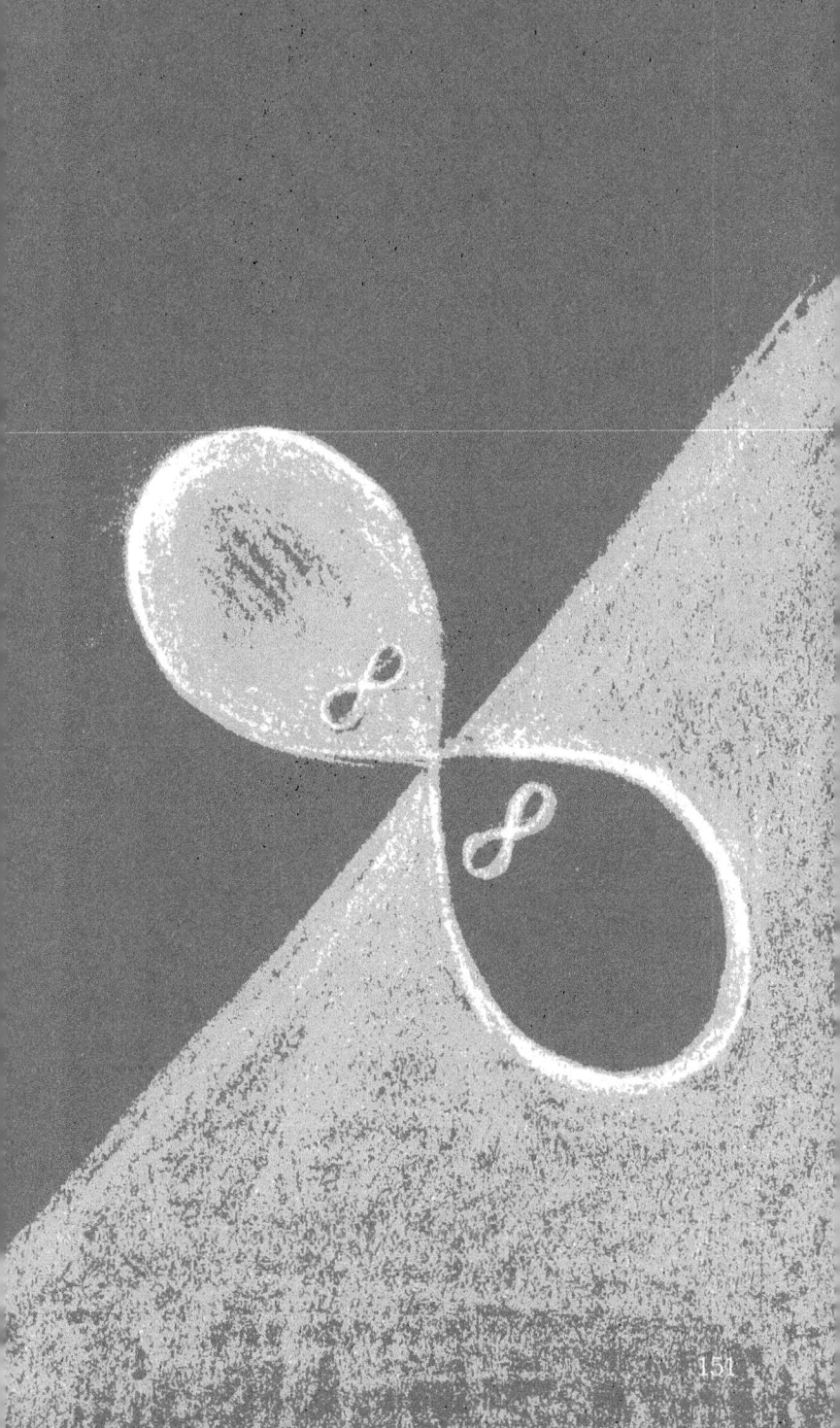

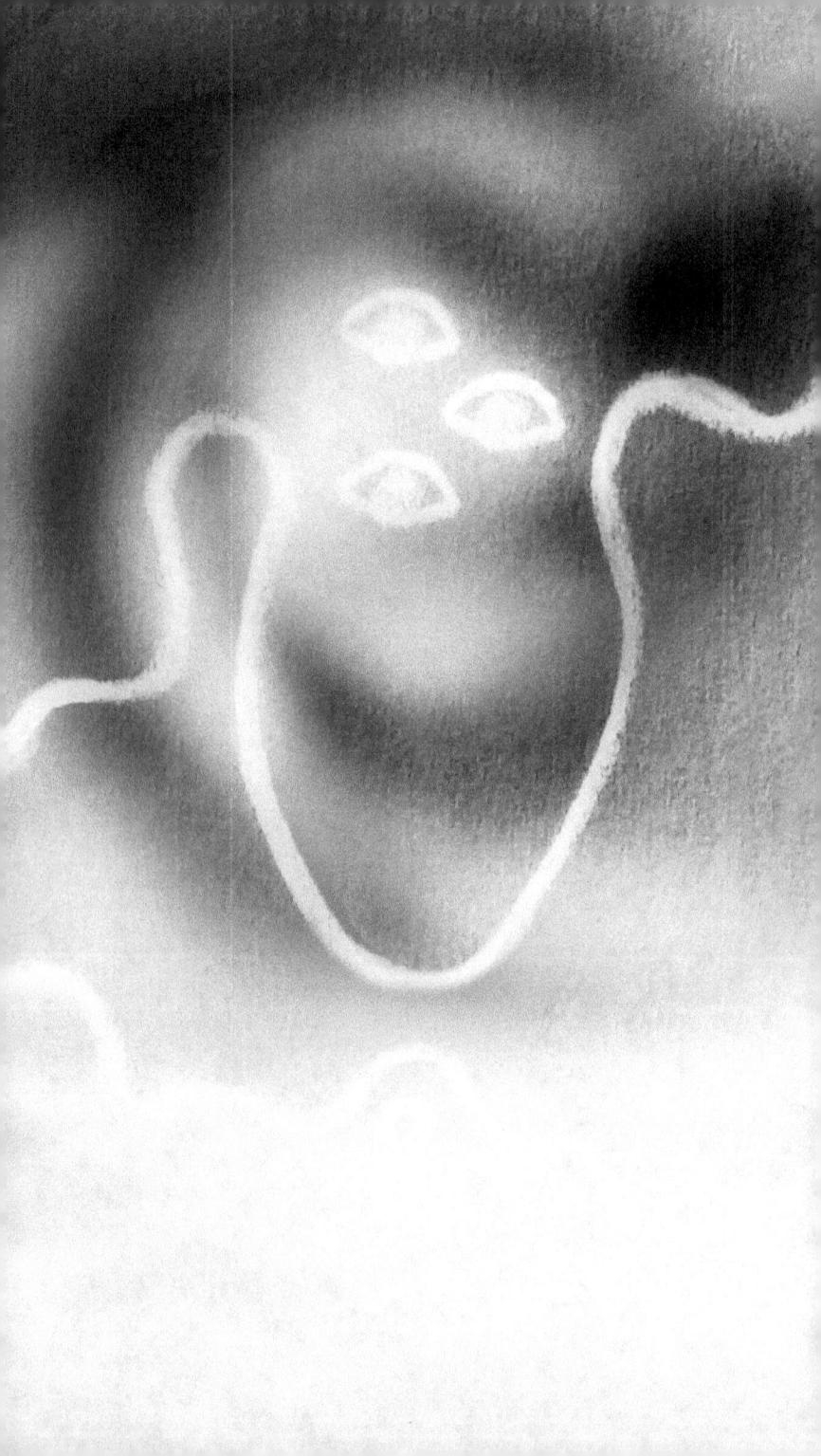

OMNIPRESENT

Where are You coming from,
Dear Lord,
and what guises are You taking on,
with these waves
that stop my thinking
and change my breathing
– turning all of me
into a spot of orgasmic pulsation?

Do not bother to answer,
just be with me for longer,
You – timeless, shapeless
yet convincingly tangible.

Do You really come and go,
or is it me who creates our encounters
by coming in and going out
of an awareness about You,
Dear Lord?

Do not bother to answer,
You, infinitely remote,
yet infinitely close,
the owner of all existence
and its essence.

REFLECTION

Thank You, Lord,
for this
sunny
cold
crystal
morning.

Thank You
for all images
that fill it in
reflecting Your perfection and serenity
throughout this moment.

Thank You
for having me
in this performance –
in which Your mighty presence,
finally acknowledged,
echoes through this I am.

SINGLE RELATIONSHIP

Only now do I clearly see
how everything in my life
has been solely one relation:
between You and me,
Dear Lord.

Other people act as Your mere representatives,
their gestures being Your responses to my
behaviour.

Beyond the apparent separation,
there is only ONE BEING,
managing its own complex ISness.

The time we surrender to the Laws of Oneness
is the time we are truly alive.

Before that stage,
life is an illusion.
Before that stage,
deprived of its spiritual energy,
our body is an illusion.

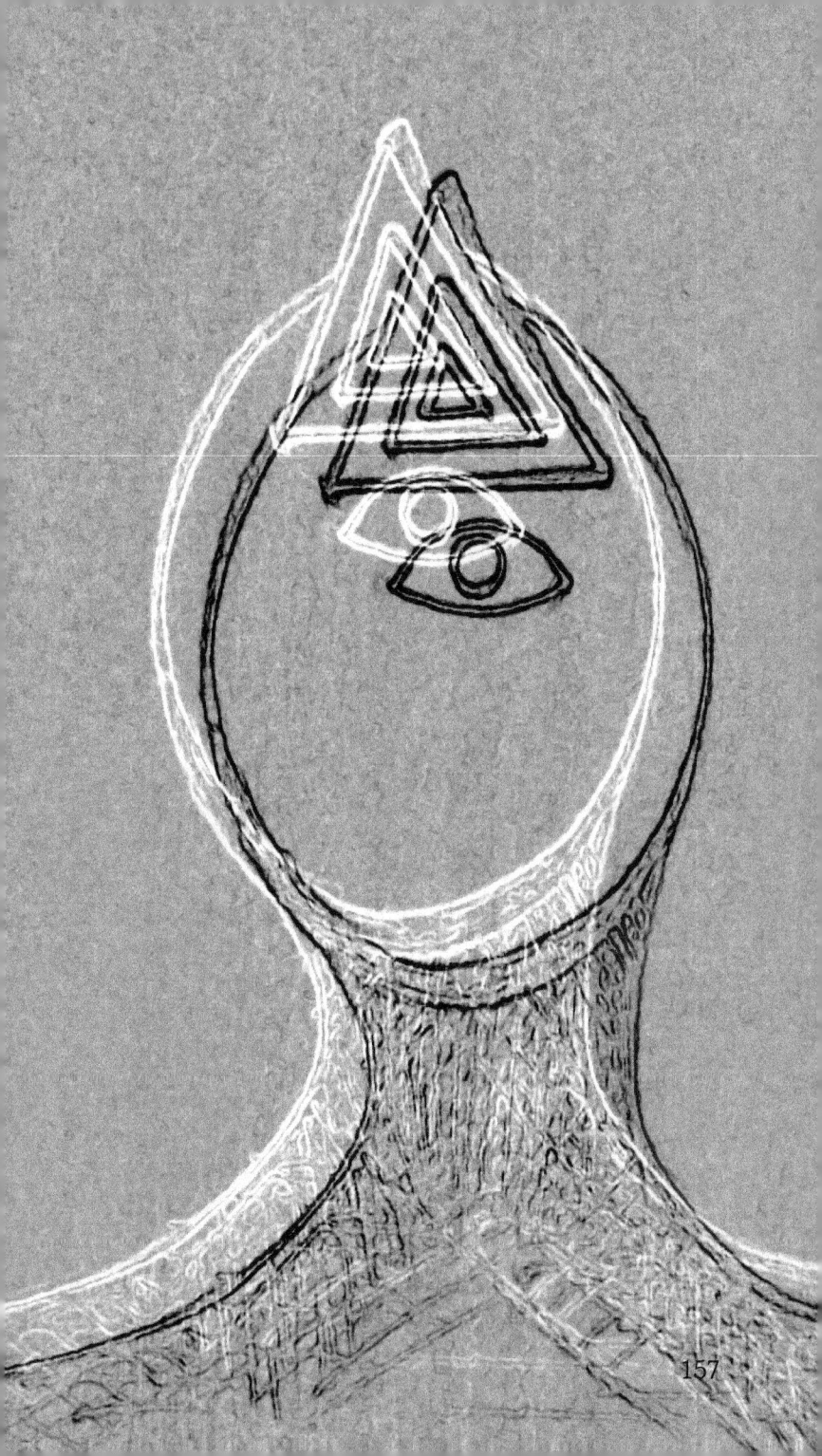

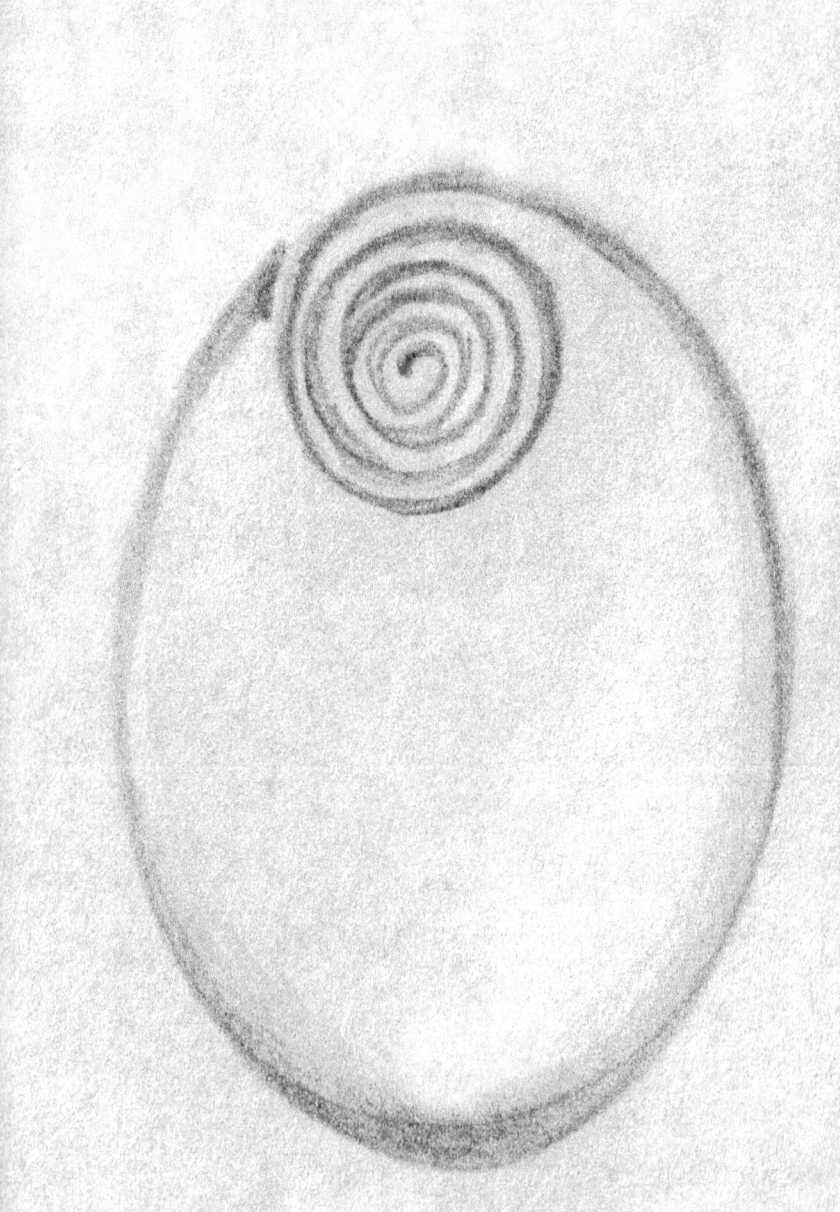

ONENESS

Whenever I am not in me
You seem nonexistent,
my Lord.

How much more
do I need to learn and grow
till the tiniest disconnection between us
becomes impossible,
till my awareness becomes fluent in divinity
and, by merging my heart and my mind,
I permanently reach
timeless beauty of Oneness?

YOU ARE THE ESSENCE

Master, my Dear,
geometrical is our relationship:
You are the essence,
You are the centre;
I am a dot revolving around You
discovering its own purpose.

No centre – no focus.
No centre – no higher meaning.
No dot – no line, no form, no geometry.

Geometry epitomises every relation,
position and meaning of every dot.
Numbers are its hidden-self.

Mathematical is my thought;
poetical is its reasoning.

What an equation
to work through!

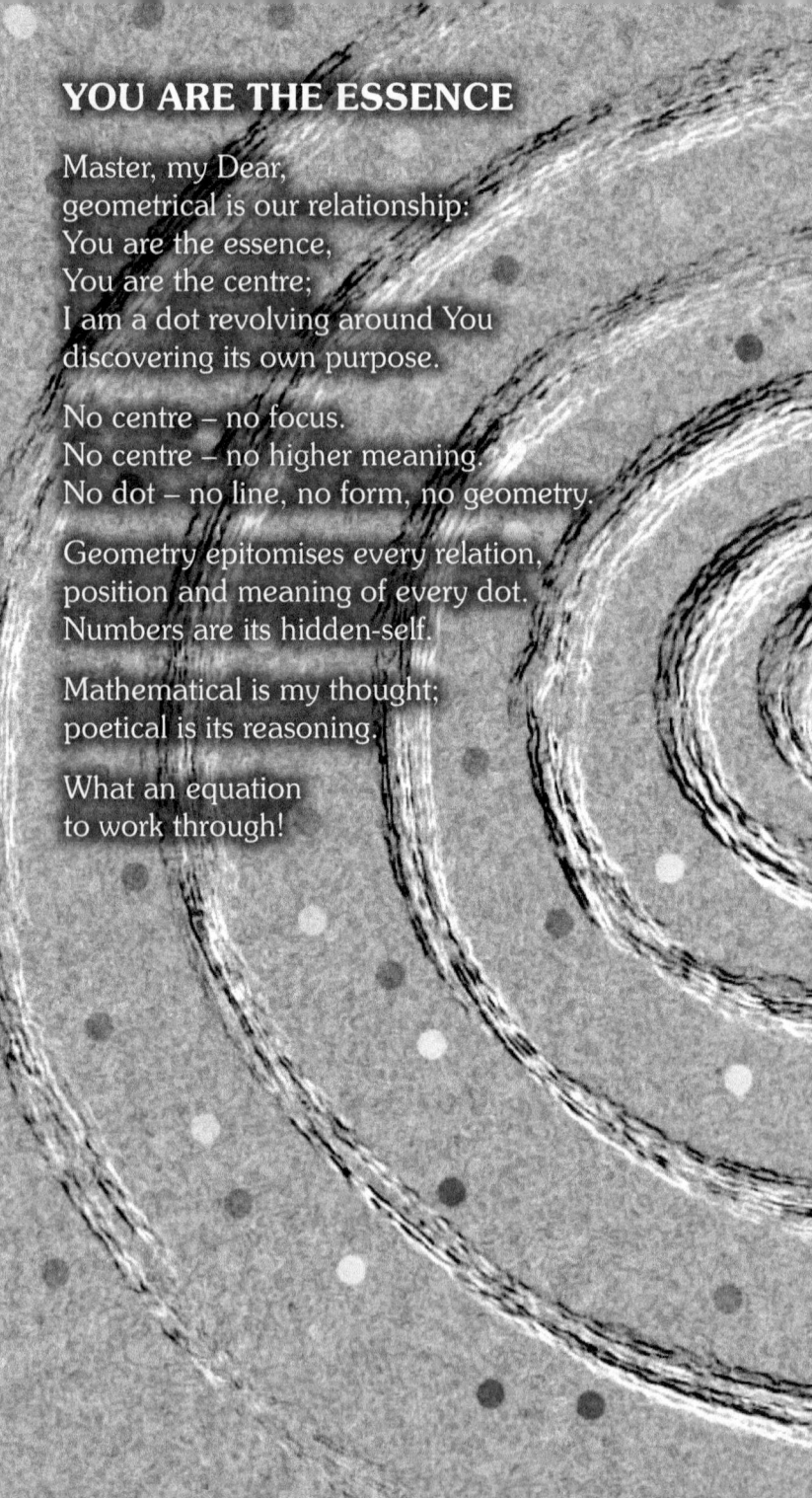

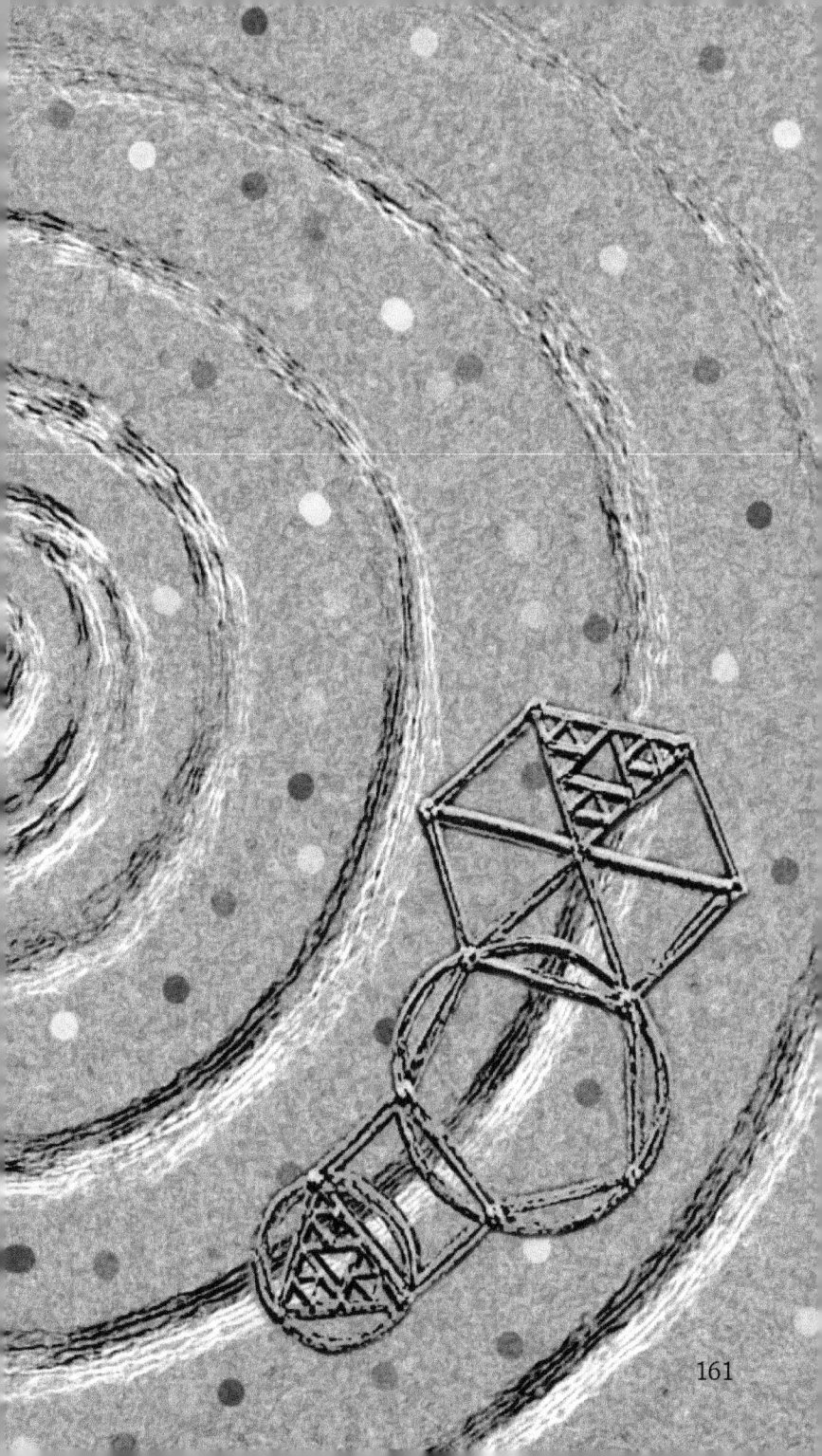

SUPREME MASTERY

And the day has come,
Dear Master,
when I want to tell You
that consciously I accept Your way.

You are not surprised by this confession. –
You programmed it into my path
and have been waiting for this moment,
patient and supportive, for time on end.

Now, through Your systems and emissaries
of the universal entourage,
You are trying to teach me
that in Your eternal vastness
everything, even my consciousness,
is the result of cosmic REFLECTIONS.

You are the greatest geometer ever –
the Owner of all dots, lines and spaces,
the Owner of times, laws and orders!

You are the greatest Master of life,
the lonely custodian of its secrets.

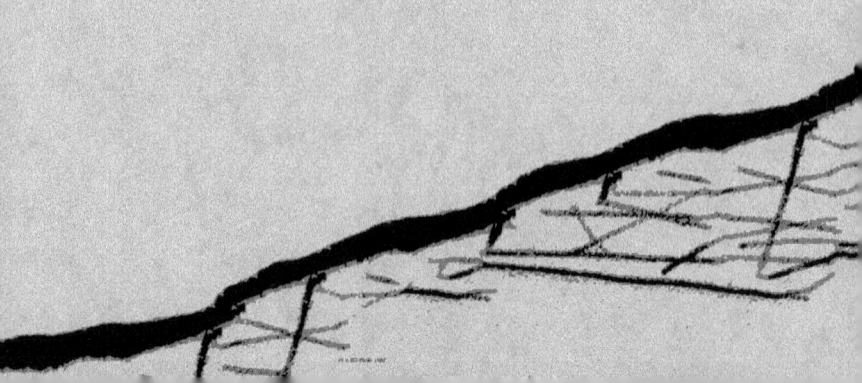

I SEE YOU INVISIBLE

This summer day,
sunny and calm,
brings You into my awareness,
so vividly, Dear Lord.

I see You basking through the invisibility of air.
I feel You mirrored in my heart.

I adore You in every flower,
in each particle that radiates its purpose
given to it by Your intent.

I know, You always wait for me
in the dimensions of
awareness and consciousness,
in infinities of two realms
– within and without.

What a way to be
You created,
my Lord!

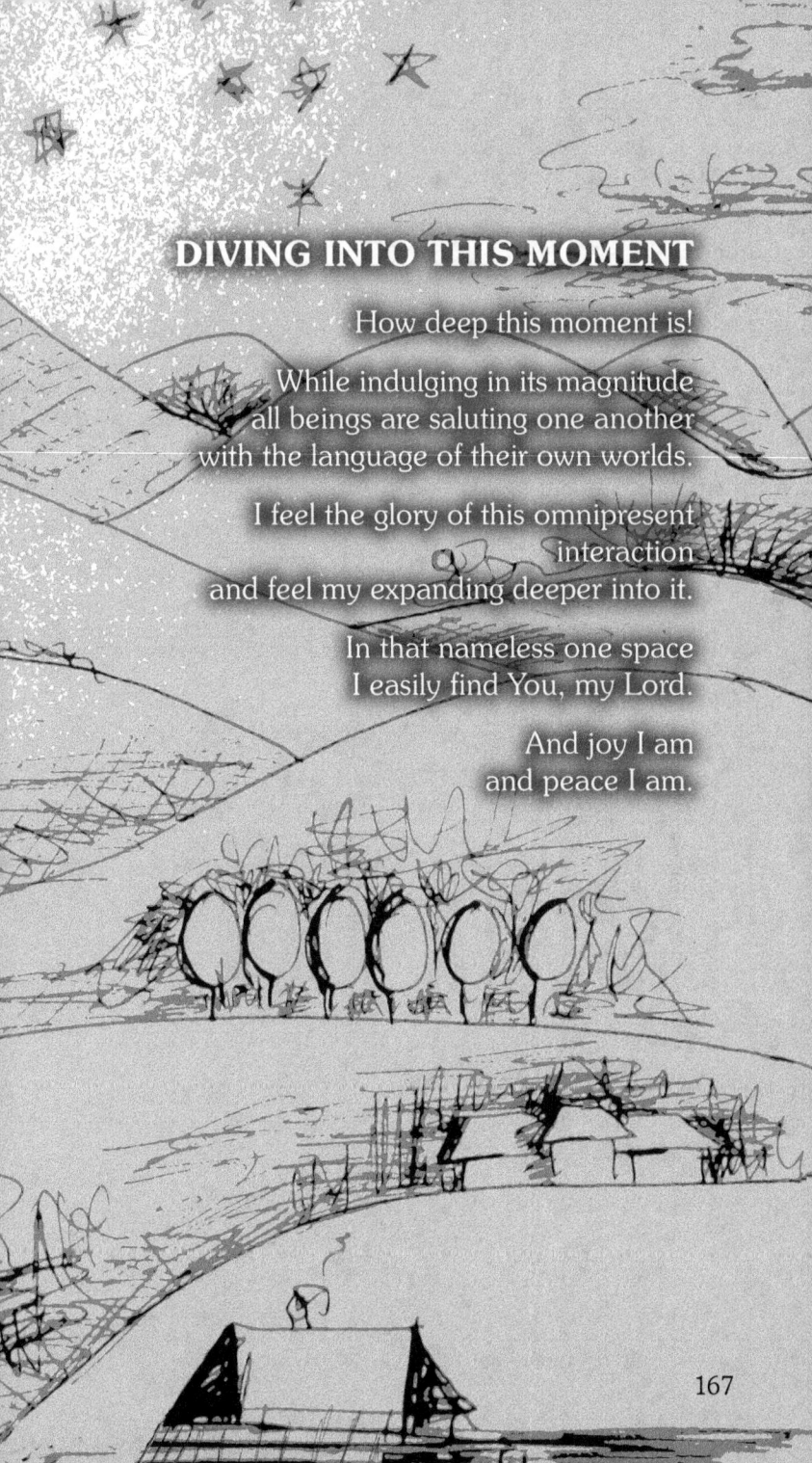

DIVING INTO THIS MOMENT

How deep this moment is!

While indulging in its magnitude
all beings are saluting one another
with the language of their own worlds.

I feel the glory of this omnipresent
interaction
and feel my expanding deeper into it.

In that nameless one space
I easily find You, my Lord.

And joy I am
and peace I am.

SOMEBODY

Somebody looks after me,
follows me;
but who it is –
I don't know.

Somebody unseen is present,
felt deeply,
somebody's love is around;
but who it is –
I don't know.

Somebody waits for me,
distant and close;
but where it is –
I don't know.

Somebody loves me,
and protects me.
I will ask my heart
who it is.

DEVOTED TO YOU

I do not await anything anymore,
Dear Lord,
because
all necessary You already gave me.

I do not need hopes anymore
because
I accept the inevitability of Your Divine Plan.

I gave up my worries
and handed them over to You
because I am entirely Yours.

I thrive on an inner knowing
of Your realness,
stamped on all of my cells –
as a primordial joy
posted to eternity.

THE LAST QUESTION

What is going on, Dear Lord,
I am living
and dying
at the same time?!

"My child,
it is to be so
till only LIGHT
remains of you."

www.ingramcontent.com/pod-product-compliance
Lightning Source LLC
LaVergne TN
LVHW051600070426
835507LV00021B/2687